Mompreneur and Dadpreneur

noun mom·pre·neur and dad·pre·neur

\'mäm-p(r)ə-'nər ən(d) 'dad-p(r)ə-'nər\

- A parent who puts their traditional, single, blended, or adoptive family first and, as a natural extension of their passion, builds business in a way that is lucrative and typically residual.

- A parent who prioritizes family and loves and trains their children with life lessons learned through family and business.

- A parent who sees the value in being a full-time family and tends to business as an extension of a mobile or home-based enterprise.

- A parent who takes a leap of faith in leaving a traditional job to make their family a priority and earns executive pay while enjoying a lifestyle of financial and time freedom for family growth.

Published by
Lessons From Network
www.LessonsFromNetwork.com

Distributed by
Lessons From Network
P.O. Box 93927
Southlake, TX 76092
817-379-2300
www.LessonsFromNetwork.com/books

ISBN: 978-0-9983125-3-8 (Paperback)

Printed in the United States of America.

Mom & Dadpreneurs

SUCCESS STORIES, STRATEGIES AND TIPS FROM SUPER ACHIEVERS IN FAMILY & BUSINESS

Join the *Mom & Dadpreneurs* Facebook Community

www.Facebook.com/MomandDadpreneurs

Share your testimonials, comments, questions, breakthroughs, successes and more.

For updates and *Mom & Dadpreneurs* news,
LIKE our page at Facebook.com/MomandDadpreneurs

Also

Receive Your Special Bonuses for Buying the *Mom & Dadpreneurs* Book

Access Multiple Free Gifts from Kelli Calabrese, Kyle Wilson and more!

Go to www.MomandDadpreneurs.com

Or send an email to
info@MomandDadpreneurs.com
With Gifts in the subject

DISCLAIMER

The information in this book is not meant to replace the advice of a medical or financial professional. Please consult a licensed physician or financial advisor in matters relating to your health and wealth particularly with respect to symptoms that may require diagnosis or medical attention or financial decisions.

If you choose to attempt any of the methods mentioned in this book, the authors and publisher advise you to take full responsibility for your safety and know your limits. The authors and publisher are not liable for any damages or negative consequences from any treatment, action, application, or preparation to any person reading or following the information in this book.

Neither the publisher nor the individual authors shall be liable for any physical, psychological, emotional, financial, or commercial damages, including, but not limited to, special, incidental, consequential, or other damages to the readers of this book.

The content of each chapter is the sole expression and opinion of its author and not necessarily that of the publisher. No warranties or guarantees are expressed or implied by the publisher's choice to include any of the content in this volume.

To order additional copies, including quantity discounts, of **Mom & Dadpreneurs** see below.

SPECIAL QUANTITY PRICING:
(Retail $17.97)

1	$12.97 ea
2-9	$9.97 ea
10-24	$6.97 ea
25-99	$5.47 ea
100+	$3.97 ea

Plus shipping. Based on location and weight.

TO ORDER PLEASE:

1. *Order online www.LessonsFromNetwork.com/Books

2. Call 817-379-2300

2. E-Mail: info@lessonsfromnetwork.com

4. Via mail: **Lessons From Network**
   P.O. Box 93927
   Southlake, TX 76092

You can mix and match these additional titles:

- *Passionistas: Tips, Tales and Tweetables From Women Pursuing Their Dreams*
- *The Little Black Book of Fitness: Breakthrough Insights from Mind, Body & Soul Warriors*
- *The Daily Difference: Life Lessons to Achieve More.*

*Order online at www.LessonsFromNetwork.com/Books and receive additional bonuses from Kelli Calabrese, Kyle Wilson and more!

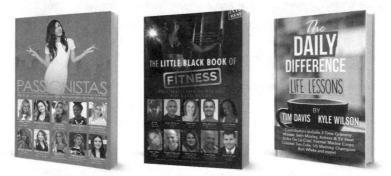

Order online www.LessonsFromNetwork.com/Books

Praise for *Mom & Dadpreneurs*

Mom & Dadpreneurs is a wonderful book, loaded with great ideas to help you build a successful family business, saving you years of hard work in achieving the same level of success.
— Brian Tracy, Author, Speaker, Consultant

I'm a believer and advocate in entrepreneurship, and I so value family! In Mom & Dadpreneurs, *Kyle Wilson, the 18 year biz partner of my mentor Jim Rohn, along with wellness professional Kelli Calabrese share powerful strategies and examples of how you can have the best of both worlds. A must read!*
— Eric Worre, Founder of NetworkMarketingPro.com, Author of #1 Bestseller *Go Pro*

Everyone's intrinsic life purpose is to have love, abundance, joy, fulfillment, and a delightful family life. It is best funded by innovative, disruptive marketing or wise Mom/Dad entrepreneurship. This book makes your trip to the good life infinitely easier when read, absorbed, and richly applied. Happy reading.
— Mark Victor Hansen, Co-creator of World's Bestselling book series, *Chicken Soup for the Soul*

Mom & Dadpreneurs shows you another way to create freedom and flexibility for your family. Yes, it is hard work, but it is not really work at all when you change people's lives.
— Kathy Coover, Owner of Isagenix

Mom & Dadpreneurs gives you clarity for leaving a legacy as parents and providers. You will be inspired to become successful familypreneurs and execute your dreams until they become a reality. These stories will encourage, motivate, and lead you to take the leap of faith to put your family first and be a super achiever in biz.
— Tony Jeary, The RESULTS Guy™

Kyle Wilson's incredible work with heavy-hitters in personal development continues to be life-changing in this collaboration with Kelli Calabrese. I know firsthand how scary it is to turn your back on the security of a 9-5 and put everything on the line to create a life where dedication to your family and passion for creating change (and income) can harmoniously coexist. The stories and lessons in this book not only give mom and dadpreneurs tools to navigate these waters, but also hope and encouragement that they are on the right path.
— Sherry Lee White, Founder & CEO of Trulee Foods, Author, Speaker

If anyone understands what it takes to be a successful entrepreneur and a world-class parent, it is Kelli Calabrese. Her ideas, tactics, and strategies will show you how to increase your earning power while raising kids who value health, contribution, and entrepreneurship.
— John Spencer Ellis, The Entrepreneur Coach

I love the idea of leaving a legacy of a passion for family and work. Living the dream of a mom and dadpreneur has the bonus of teaching kids about business as a part of everyday life. The world needs more familypreneurs!
— Holly Homer, Author of *The 101 Coolest Simple Science Experiments* and Blogger of Kids Activities Blog

After reading a few pages of this stunning book, I knew that this book was not only a special read, but it was also so full of powerful tips and secrets of success, that the only word I could think of was ACCELERATOR. It will accelerate and activate every aspect of your life and business with these stories, and do it quickly. This book screams GENIUS.
— Dr. Doug Firebaugh, Christian, Father, Husband, Home Business Entrepreneur, Author, and Host of the National Radio Show "The Millionaire Road"

How do you create a lasting legacy? Start by showing your kids the real world possibilities for their future. In this inspiring book, you'll find amazing stories from incredible parents who have found a way to include balance inside of business. Read it now! Your family's future may depend on it.
— Robert Helms, Real Estate Investor and Developer and Host of The Real Estate Guys™ Radio & Television Programs

This is the kind of book I wish I had when I decided to quit my job to start my own business and be home with my kids and everyone was telling me I was crazy. Mom & Dadpreneurs *debunks the myth that raising a family and having a successful home-based is impossible. Each story gives hope, inspiration, and tools to moms and dads who know there's a better way outside the corporate walls. A must read.*
— Jackie VanCampen, Bestselling Author, Speaker, and Breakthrough Facilitator

As a career corporate executive, I understand the drive to excel professionally and also the tug on your heart to be with your children. Mom & Dadpreneurs *shares stories of moms and dads like me who figured out a way to enjoy that sweet spot between personal and professional life. It's a must read for parents.*
— Ginger Mollo, Sr. Director Operations L&D at Apple Inc

Being mom and dadpreneurs has afforded my family and I the freedom to grow closer together and unlock the financial blueprint that we desired. There's nothing else like it! Kelli Calabrese paints a brilliant picture of this in Mom & Dadpreneurs.
— Alvie Shepherd, Former MLB player for the Baltimore Orioles

Yes, you can live a purpose-filled life, prioritize family, achieve financial and time freedom, while pursuing passions and life priorities! In Mom & Dadpreneurs, *authors Kelli Calabrese and Kyle Wilson provide dozens of inspirational success stories along with personal insight, experience, and valuable suggestions. Kelli and Kyle are passionate, effective leaders, developing a new generation of collaborative, purpose-filled entrepreneurs. I'm honored by their friendship and blessed by their mentorship!*
— Tim Cole, Colonel USMC Ret

Mom & Dadpreneurs *is a wonderful example of balancing parenthood and entrepreneurship at its best! This book is a must read for my two daughters, three stepdaughters, and five son-in-laws. Each and every story is an inspiration of determination, true grit, and love.*
— Ron Jones, Author and Consultant

Mom & Dadpreneurs *is an amazingly inspiring book about family-focused entrepreneurs who make life and work happen in concert with one another. You will find the stories and testimonies shared in* Mom & Dadpreneurs *to be inspiring, authentic, and catalytic for personal connection and action.*
— Jim Gardner, Owner and Coach, Elite Performance Fit

Foreword

by Tom Ziglar

Question: What would you do if a good friend of over 20 years who you had done numerous deals with that all turned out better than he promised, asked you to read a book he strongly believed in and write a foreword for it? You would do it! Just as I expected, Kyle Wilson has once again exceeded my expectation.

Kyle is masterful at finding talent and harnessing it. His entire career he has surrounded himself with experts in all industries and co-created legacy products. In *Mom & Dadpreneurs* he teamed up with wellness expert, trainer, and coach Kelli Calabrese, and together they collaborated on what will be more than a revelatory book, but a movement. Kelli's heart to help more parents work from home so they can tend to their family inspired the book.

Mom & Dadpreneurs is a unique collection of self-written stories by people real people like you and me who determined to take a greater than-typical role in parenting and dedicate as much of their time as possible to growing strong, healthy families. Interestingly enough, these efforts resulted in their becoming financially stable and even exceptionally so. In nearly all cases, they have overcome some pretty difficult circumstances to turn their lives around. These people are very open about their struggles and excited about sharing their experiences in an effort to encourage and motivate others who have the inclination to do so. No matter where you are in your own life story, there is information in this book that can benefit you in improving most of the circumstances of your own life. I believe it's a "must read" for anyone searching for "more."

Tom Ziglar – CEO of Ziglar Inc

TABLE OF CONTENTS

Foreword
    By Tom Ziglar 9

Introduction
    By Kelli Calabrese 13

Chapter 1: The Moment My Heart Forever Shifted
    By Kelli Calabrese 15

Chapter 2: Failed Swiss Startup Sparks Lifestyle Investing Success
    By Michael Brownell 21

Chapter 3: From Business Suits to Yoga Pants: A Bumpy Journey to Time Freedom and Financial Abundance
    By Laura Hernandez 25

Chapter 4: #BossMomma From Welfare to Wealth
    By Rachell Brinkerhoff 31

Chapter 5: From My Parents' Basement to Two Grammys
    By Seth Mosley 37

Chapter 6: The Birth of a New Family
    By Mark and Tamiel Kenney 43

Chapter 7: #BucketListGoalCrusher
    By Dawn Cermak 47

Chapter 8: Claiming My Worth: Becoming a Millionaire Mom on a Mission
    By Janine Brolly 53

Chapter 9: Our Journey of Healing, Family, and Hope
    By Scott and Susan Wooley 57

Chapter 10: The Re-Defined American Dream
    By Ed and Bessie Goldin 61

Chapter 11: Giving Your Best in the Most Difficult Times
    By Gbenga Asedeko 65

Chapter 12: It's Not About the Position: It's About the Mission
    By Taylor Thompson 69

Chapter 13: A Life of Simple Choices
By Todd Falcone 75

Chapter 14: Paratroopers Turned Full-Time Family
By Daniel and Tara Parten. 81

Chapter 15: Freaky Friday
By Joanne Moretti 85

Chapter 16: Brave and Passionate: A Better Life for My Girls
By Angela Maresca 89

Chapter 17: The Opportunity to Leave a Legacy
By Ron Miller 93

Chapter 18: Broken Mom and Broken Back to Super Mom and Super Fit
By Sarah Rhew 97

Chapter 19: Courage Beyond the Lies
By Barb Nicholson. 103

Chapter 20: Escaping the Phone Book: Breaking out of the Box!
By Laurel Boylan 109

Chapter 21: From Beer Money to Successful Faith-Driven Mompreneur
By Brenda Fenner 113

Chapter 22: How I Ended My Life to Find My DRIVE
By Melissa Kirkpatrick 119

Chapter 23: Parenting Through the Eyes of Faith
By Gary and Cindy Mejia. 123

Chapter 24: The Stolen Family: How They Slip Away One Thought at a Time
By Sean G. Murphy 129

Chapter 25: Purpose Led Profit
By Donna Krech 133

Chapter 26: Leaving the World Better Than When We Found It
By Simon Chan 137

Chapter 27: Finding Your Path
By Kyle Wilson 143

Additional Information 149

About the Author 152

Dedication

To my friend and soul sister, Michelle Weaver, who taught me about the supernatural power of a family through her personal walk with her husband and my mentor, Kevin Weaver, and their three amazing children, Olivia, Noah, and Manny. This is one of the many books to be written as fruit from your teachings!

To every child, this book is for you and your families. You are worthy, you are important, and you are loved.

To my parents who were serial entrepreneurs and set the stage for hard work, ingenuity, and always making family a priority.

To my husband, Anthony, who makes it known daily how much he loves me and our children and who has supported this book and every one of my projects for the past 25 years. And to my extraordinary children, Nicholas and Melina, who I do my best to set an example for, may you walk in confidence, grounded in who you are, moving towards love's ideal in every situation until it's a present tense reality.

To the moms and dads who want more out of life, may this open up new possibilities for you to follow your dreams to be loving parents and super achievers in the business that your heart desires. May this inspire and equip you to live your dreams. It is possible.

Acknowledgement

To Kyle Wilson, the master marketer, promoter, coach, mentor, and leader who over delivers, leads with his heart, is an extraordinary networker, is purpose-filled, passionate, formulaic, and constantly upping his game, thank you for believing in me and inviting me to partner with you on this book, which will become a movement, changing countless families and positioning them for exponential love and growth!

Takara Sights, you are an editing maven. Thank you for being an exceptional project manager and editor. You made the process of coordinating dozens of co-authors effortless. Blessings, friend!

Introduction

by Kelli Calabrese

Through a God-coincidence, I was invited to be part of Kyle Wilson's Inner Circle Mastermind. Kyle was the behind-the-scenes guy, the masterful promoter who founded Jim Rohn International and was Jim's partner for 18 years filling rooms with people seeking personal development and betterment in life. He promoted the likes of Brian Tracy, Mark Victor Hansen, and other leaders in personal development you would recognize.

I knew Kyle and his group were special super achievers with heart. At the end of the first day, he looked me in the eyes and said, "You have a book in you. Is it a fitness book?" Knowing I had 30+ years experience in the fitness, wellness, and nutrition industry he figured it was a natural "yes." My answer was a quick no. I had written fitness books before. I had an idea for my next book but asked him if I could sleep on the answer before responding.

That night I received a very clear impression of what the book was to be about. I had just spent the day with my sweet friend Michelle Weaver who was in her final moments of a four-year horrific battle with cancer. She was leaving behind three precious children ages 8 to 14. It was heartbreaking to know her time on Earth was short, but what I did know was in the years she had with her children, they were "discipled up." They were strong in every area of their lives, joy-filled, healthy, confident in who they were, and while they would grieve and miss their mom, they would be strengthened in every way because they were kingdom-minded.

In that same week, a 13-year-old girl in our neighborhood tried to take her life. In my soul, I knew that was unacceptable, and I didn't want another child to feel unworthy or unloved.

I called Kyle and told him my heart to help moms and dads be a full-time family first, tending to their passions and business as a natural extension of family life. He said, "Oh, like a Mom and Dadpreneur," and so, the title was birthed.

Since my son was born 17 years ago and I left my company, I have figured out a way to be with him and my daughter and also earn the executive pay I had become accustomed to. It didn't happen in an instant, but knowing what I now know, and through the stories of these co-authors, you can see it's possible for anyone, and you can accelerate your results having read these stories.

Each of these contributors wants you to be your best following your passions and your talents and for your family to get the best of you, not the leftovers or the worst of you. I prayed for the right contributors to present themselves for the book, the ones whose stories would be compelling and speak to parents in a variety of situations regardless of being a traditional family, blended, single, or adoptive.

Each of the contributors is vulnerable. They tell the hard things. Even the secret things. It's difficult to have a favorite story as each person's walk is unique and will speak to your heart. There were fears, challenges to overcome, setbacks and uncertainty to be endured. Every one of these co-authors is an overcomer. From immigrating to a new country to being saddled with debt, to those with unemployment, abuse, addiction, illness, language barriers, depression, lawsuits, pride, and in some cases success, these parents did what was best for their family and are better for it.

I encourage you to read every story, and as you do, compile a list of people who come to mind who need to read these stories. As they are highlighted to you, write their name on the inside back cover and consider paying it forward by sharing copies of this book with other parents you know who want betterment in their families. This is for those who want to live without the guilt of missing the important times, without fear of someone else raising your child with their values, without the anger, exhaustion, or desperation of how to get out of the rat race and with freedom of time and money. That's why we have special pricing for you when you buy this book in quantities of 10 or more.

Let's make this a movement in giving parents hope and practical ways they can become mom and dadpreneurs, being their own bosses, raising future entrepreneurs, parenting successfully, positively influencing children as you groom the next generation of world changers and unemployable millionaires. This book can make that kind of a difference.

CHAPTER 1

The Moment My Heart Forever Shifted

by Kelli Calabrese

I was not the girl who grew up playing with dolls and wishing upon becoming a mommy. I loved being physically active and was a Type A action taker. I grew up in a family of entrepreneurs with a furious work ethic and started working in the family business at age 11. By 17, I secured a job I was passionate about in a health club. I quickly worked my way from receptionist to leading fitness classes. While completing three science degrees including a master's in clinical exercise physiology and cardiac rehabilitation, I progressed from becoming a fitness trainer to, ultimately, a co-owner. Over a 14-year period, my partners and I opened up a chain of four health clubs and managed corporate fitness centers for companies such as Calvin Klein and Beneficial Insurance. I co-founded the first school to prepare candidates to become certified fitness professionals and had several hundred employees and thousands of members to tend to.

I loved it. Working and growing a fitness business was my heart, soul, and life at the time. That was the point when, after seven years of marriage to my amazing husband Anthony, we were pregnant with our son Nicholas. I put on my to-do list to check out a new daycare in town, took a tour, and enrolled him before he took his first breath. I remember being impressed that I could watch my infant son from a monitor at work and believed that was reassuring.

Then Nicholas was born. Six weeks later, I sat in the daycare center staring into his big, brown eyes, about to lay his tiny body in a crib for the first time. I couldn't do it. That was the moment everything changed. My heart forever shifted. I knew I could not leave him there. My husband and I were to be the primary givers of care, the ones to lead him, love him, influence him, and be connected heart to heart.

I walked out, called Anthony, and told him there was going to be another way. I had no idea what that was, but we were going to figure it out. I worked when he napped or when family could be with him. Within a few months, I was pregnant with our daughter Melina, and I knew the life of a health club owner was not going to fit the mommy life I wanted. I still was not a gushy, head-over-heels mom, as the magnetism to work was what energized me, but I knew it was time for a new season.

Thankfully, my partner was able to buy me out. I remember coming home, sitting at my desk with my newborn and a baby in my belly and wondering what I would do. My spirit and identity were in my work, and I was feeling ripped out of my world.

A door opened. I applied to become the lead fitness expert for eDiets. They were the largest online diet subscription based website, and they wanted me to develop their fitness portal from home. Then I was invited to edit our industry's leading magazine...from home. I decided to create a women's fitness program that included a book, workbook, journal, and audio programs all from home.

Still having a heart to be connected to my industry and help fitness trainers raise their level of professionalism, I began speaking at industry events. I was also invited to host media tours. I started online wellness coaching and running a fitness boot camp that allowed me to be home by 7 a.m. before my family woke up. My priorities were to be full-time, family first and still be a super achiever making an impact in my industry and on anyone willing to listen about becoming well.

In 2010, I was introduced to a wellness network marketing company that was in alignment with my beliefs and mission. I became a top achiever, and it added financial freedom that took our lifestyle and generosity to a new level. For the first time, I could help other parents have the same familypreneur lifestyle. That excited me! At no time since I made the decision to become a mompreneur was there an ounce of regret. I have had the opportunity to be available for my family and earn executive pay. My children have seen mom grow personally and professionally, speak in front of groups and achieve big goals. They have the opportunity to meet interesting, successful, and influential people who visit our home from around the world. From an early age, they were a part of planning events, enjoying earned trips, and they have also seen disappointment, which is all a part of life, parenting, and entrepreneurship.

In 2015, my dad's health was failing. I was able to travel from Dallas to New Jersey 14 times to visit him and help my mom. Without the freedom of time and money, I would not have been able to do that. Many times I brought my children with me to spend last, precious moments with my dad and support my mom. I never had to check in with a boss, apply for time off, or use a vacation day. I was paid every day!

Recently, I asked my son what one of his hardest days was, and he said saying goodbye to papa that last time. They both knew it was probably the last time they would see each other. They had long stares, my dad imparted some wisdom on him, Nicholas hugged his frail body, and it made a lasting impression. Being a mompreneur allowed that moment to happen.

Is being a mompreneur perfect? Never! Not even remotely close! We have made plenty of mistakes. We've missed the mark too many times to count. There are multitudes of things I wish I had done differently. However, through the tough times (unemployment, a lawsuit, broken bones, a cross-country move, surgeries, floods, hail damage, car accidents, a homeschool fail, head injuries, failed businesses, financial issues, death, and disappointment) we choose to stick together, support each other, learn from every situation, and find a way to have more excellent outcomes.

My friends Kevin and Michelle Weaver shared with me their definition of love. Love is contending for the highest possible good in every situation until it's a present tense reality. We all make mistakes, we all fall short, but we continue to love. That's the rule in our family. There is supernatural power to a united, loving family. In our family, we allow ourselves to dream big, experience adventures, and not helicopter parent. We set our family up for success, allow for failure, endure the consequences, and come out better for it. We encourage our kids with core values that inspire them to seek God first, have servant hearts, set and exceed goals, be intentional in their actions, take responsibility, and hold high expectations for their life's purpose. We love them on purpose and look for teaching moments on principles such as faith, health, integrity, gratitude, leadership development, and fun.

One exercise we like to do with our children is to teach them to dream. Since my daughter was three years old she has been talking about being a veterinarian. She has a vivid image of what her ranch will look like including her house, barn, clinic, photography studio, pet cemetery, guest house, and landing strip for when she gets to rescue animals. She has drawn her ranch out on poster board, shared the dream with people she meets, and is working towards making that happen. She has spent days at a veterinary clinic and spends any spare moments at a barn where she rides horses, trains puppies, and helps out with grooming, feeding, maintenance, and horse camps. She also is a competitive equestrian! We agree with her and believe this dream is possible.

In the short-term, it would be easier to let our kids go to aftercare, book their calendar with activities, and be raised without technology limits. In the long-term, by having a heart-to-heart connection and in giving kids your best, you are building happy, healthy, responsible, confident children who you can enjoy a long-term relationship with regardless of their choices.

Another thing we do as a family is create vision boards so we know each other's intentions and how we can support them. It's a powerful family exercise. We also keep a gratitude jar in the kitchen and record what we are grateful for along with the date. We read the year's worth of gratitude notes on New Year's Eve. It's another insight into each other's hearts.

Understanding and using each others' love languages (from the book *The 5 Love Languages*) has also served our family. It's helped us to realize that the way we feel loved is not necessarily how others do and we can modify our styles to make the person feel loved. If I could turn back time I would have more pillow talk at night and listen to their dreams. I would have more table time, family game nights, outdoor adventures, individual dates, journaling, more down time, and more acts of service. I would ask the hard questions and answer the hard questions.

There were times when my children made choices about serving or comforting a friend or taking the road less popular that I take no credit for. I know they were being led by a power within them greater than I could teach them. I'm thankful to co-labor with a higher power while I have the privilege of intentionally parenting them for a brief time. Our desire is for our children to be equipped to make a kingdom impact during their time on earth. We want them to lead joy-filled lives as difference makers, poised for the challenges that life is bound to throw them and grateful for every opportunity to grow spiritually, physically, financially, emotionally, relationally, socially, and professionally.

Taking the step of faith to be mom and dadpreneurs was no accident. It was not always easy, but is definitely worth it. I have never desired one time to wake up in the morning by an alarm clock, put on a suit, drop my kids off at school, commute downtown for an hour to sit in a cubicle at a job I hate, hoping for a two percent raise and an extra day's vacation, with my spouse and children getting the worst of me. My family does not get the leftovers of my energy, patience, thinking, time, creativity, or love. Being a wife and a full-time mom is a responsibility I take seriously. It's also helped me learn to laugh more! I encourage you to find a way to let your family be your priority, to have the best of you. It's never too late regardless of what phase of parenting or grandparenting you are in.

TWEETABLE

There's nothing you can do to make me love you more.
There's nothing you can do to make me love you less.

Kelli Calabrese is a 31-year fitness, nutrition, and lifestyle coach. She has owned and operated health clubs and managed corporate fitness centers. She was the lead fitness expert for eDiets and Montel Williams, and was interviewed by NBC for the lead trainer on The Biggest Loser. *She has been voted personal trainer of the year three times, was the editor of* Personal Fitness Professional *magazine, and has appeared on NBC, ABC, CBS, and FOX affiliates speaking on fitness, nutrition, and wellness topics. Kelli is a top achiever with Isagenix and is committed to helping people be a full-time family while earning executive pay and having a lifestyle of freedom.*

This wellness mompreneur encourages people to be their best—spirit, mind, and body. Through her speaking, books, and solutions, she inspires you to enjoy a fit, energized body, sharp mind, and joy-filled lifestyle. She encourages everyone to be purpose-filled parents.

www.KelliCalabrese.com
Facebook: Kelli Calabrese
Twitter: Kelli Calabrese
Kelli@KelliCalabrese.com
469-744-9154

CHAPTER 2

Failed Swiss Startup Sparks Lifestyle Investing Success

by Michael Brownell

"Honey, what do you think about moving to Switzerland? An interesting opportunity has come up." My wife, Nancy, looked up at me with that mix of humor, surprise, and concern that greets many of my "great ideas."

"Let's talk about it," she said, "over a glass of wine, after we put the kids to bed."

As a paperboy in middle school, I'd learned the fundamentals of being an entrepreneur: delivering a quality product and service, taking care of customers, and generating profits. I used these principles to pay my way through college in a variety of ventures including a car detailing business and as a freelance cabinet installer. I loved the lifestyle of flexible work and income while being a student. During college, I found physics and lasers as a passion and thought high-tech looked like a great career path. It was exciting to think about getting into the professional ranks and experiencing the next phase of adult life.

Armed with an advanced degree in an emerging technology, I headed out into the world of entrepreneurial startup companies in the Silicon Valley. It was exciting. And hard. There were lots of smart, motivated people, and I made lots of new friends. It required high levels of perseverance and stamina. It's a rewarding and challenging roller coaster ride. A lot like life.

Nancy and I first met in high school but were in different social circles. Some time after the 10-year reunion (where we actually danced on the tables together) we got together, married, and had kids. She was a primary care physician with a nice practice, and I was an entrepreneur with some good early-stage company experience. Life was good. But we were super busy, I was traveling a lot for work, and we wanted to have more time with the kids. Nancy began scaling back to part time. It's difficult to balance work and family and life.

So, after putting the kids to bed and opening a nice bottle of wine, we talked about Switzerland on the patio of our southern California home. Living in Switzerland sounded really exciting. The opportunity was with a startup company developing a laser technology, right up my alley, and I knew the founders from a previous venture.

Nancy couldn't practice medicine in Europe, so she would be a full-time mom, which was fine with her. We love Europe and traveling so that was a big plus. Our children, Adam and Rachel, were ages six and five, so they'd be fine with it.

But then there is the risk the company would fail. Most startups do. What then? We'd be leaving our friends and family and familiarity and moving to the other side of the planet. What would life be like? After some time thinking it through, we decided to go for it. It's a big life decision, and an interesting feeling when a shipping container with all your possessions leaves on a flatbed truck to travel by ship to a different continent. It's a little scary. I had a new view of our "stuff" after that. It's just stuff. My family was the real treasure.

The Swiss and European lifestyle was great. The food, the people, the architecture, the history. The travel and cultural experiences. Really fun. The startup was fascinating, and I was working a lot, but the Swiss have a much different work style than Silicon Valley. It's a culture of excellence and precision and strong work ethic, but also one of ensuring there is personal time and a quality of life. Very different from California, but very refreshing. We were learning a new way of life with a family and lifestyle focus.

The company was hitting its milestones, and the technology worked. But after two years the market had imploded. The business plan got crushed and the company was out of money. The startup had failed. I had moved my family to Europe and had lost my job. It wasn't clear what we should do. Things were confusing and uncertain. Moving back to California was an option, so was looking for something in Europe. Either way I'd have to start a job search, and we may have to move again to another country. These are the times you really question yourself and your path.

The search for answers was murky, and there were some dark days. I was used to this process in my professional life as an entrepreneur. In a startup company you are always venturing into the unknown with a vision and perseverance, figuring things out along the way. But this felt more personal. These were huge life decisions that really impacted our family. How would I balance that? The risks seemed high, and I felt exposed. I came to realize that all my entrepreneurial efforts had always gone into my professional life, but I hadn't leveraged that thinking into my personal life, or into my investments. Interesting.

At that time I found the book *Rich Dad Poor Dad* by Robert Kiyosaki and had an epiphany. You could be an entrepreneur with your investments. You could seek out passive cash flow from real estate to replace or augment your income. You could create your own family business that supports your lifestyle. Be a family entrepreneur. During this time I had found another early phase company opportunity in England, and we moved there. But now I had a parallel mission: to seek out and build a family business focused on passive cash flow investing that would directly support our family lifestyle.

I wrote a business plan, like I'd done several times for tech companies, but this time it was for our personal business and family goals. Soon, I was a Californian living in England and buying my first multifamily property in Alabama. Somehow this made perfect sense. It was a 10-unit complex I'd found on a scouting trip there that fit the model I'd built in our plan.

We continued looking and investing in multifamily properties for the next several years, and also moved back to California. Nancy had studied law online while we were in Europe and passed the bar after moving back, so she handled the legal side of the business. We've since ventured into other asset classes like commercial and resort properties. We focus on what we call lifestyle investing: integrating your lifestyle interests into smart cash flowing investments. It's an entrepreneurial family business.

Our kids have grown up watching us build it, participating in it, and taking family trips where we have adventures and look at investments. Now they are in college and have an entrepreneurial mindset in their approach and a sensible view of personal finance, which they got from our family businesses, not the school system. Nancy and I have become empty nesters and are even more focused on our lifestyle investments, with a fresh vision for putting our family first and bringing opportunities to friends and fellow investors. We love travel, scuba diving, snow skiing, and time with friends, so we've incorporated that into our business strategy by finding good investments in places that fit our lifestyle, like the Caribbean and the mountains. Our friends and like-minded people participate in these investments along with us, as we all put paradise in our portfolios. Even our aging parents have inspired us to look into senior housing as an investment with family in mind.

So, moving the family to Switzerland for a startup company turned out to be a great move, but not for the reasons we thought. The company failed. But, it led us to become family entrepreneurs and to focus on lifestyle investing. And my family is still the real treasure.

TWEETABLE

Joining a startup in Switzerland was life-changing. The company failed, but we became family entrepreneurs focused on lifestyle investing.

Michael and Nancy Brownell continue consulting in their professional fields as well as making lifestyle investments and sponsoring syndications in income producing real estate. These investments now include vacation property, coffee farms, apartments, and senior housing. They welcome opportunities to connect with like-minded people who are interested in investing alongside them for passive cash flow and lifestyle freedom. Reach Michael at michael1brownell@gmail.com, on Facebook, or LinkedIn.

CHAPTER 3

From Business Suits to Yoga Pants
A Bumpy Journey to Time Freedom and Financial Abundance

by Laura Hernandez

Like many, I went to college for four years in pursuit of a career that would allow me the American dream. Not knowing I had options, I completed six years in university to obtain my BA and MBA and then another two years to obtain my CPA license. And so, I officially joined the "rat race." For 15 years I worked my way up in accounting to become the CFO of a large public company, and I thought I had "made it." I wore the nicest business suits, donning pencil skirts with high heels everyday, and sat in a corner office overlooking the bay, watching boats sail by. I was content, although I always secretly wanted to be out on the water instead of at my desk. It was a great job that allowed me certain luxuries such as owning a condo at the beach, driving a Mercedes, and hosting parties every weekend. I was single and having fun, but I still had to report to work for someone else every Monday morning and ask permission for any time off.

My priorities quickly started to change when I met my husband. I met Rick as a successful banker. He was kind, sweet, and funny, and we were engaged within a year. We got married, and went to Maui on our honeymoon. We didn't know it then, but our adventures on The Road to Hana blessed us with our first little girl, Hana Love, born exactly nine months after my wedding week. Having her changed everything for us, and our priorities and life plans began to evolve. We never knew that type of love existed, and we both started to become better people because of her.

At the time, my boss had given me three months of maternity leave, but he called me back into work at the two-month mark. I was devastated to have to leave my brand new baby, but I felt I didn't have a choice and was grateful to even have a good job in what people started to call "the recession."

A year later, we took our first date trip to NYC since we'd had our first child, and we stayed on Madison Avenue—exactly nine months later, our second angel would be born and named Madison, of course. We were ecstatic to discover we were having a second child, however, my boss wasn't.

He couldn't imagine having to pay me for another two months while I was not working, and so he laid me off while I was pregnant "because of the recession." We were living in the nicest part of town, drove two luxury cars, were very social, traveled often, and now had two babies. So, the thought of possibly having to sacrifice any of that drove me to start my own accounting practice that took off quickly. Having my own business gave me some of the freedom that I was seeking, however, missing my older daughter's first preschool ballet recital, because I was at the mercy of my client's deadlines was a reality check.

Traditional self-employment, whether brick-and-mortar or service, does afford some freedoms, but it still requires having to answer to clients/customers/employees. I started to imagine that there had to be a better way to create a LIFE by my own design, instead of just making a living. I just didn't know how—yet.

I was waking up and heading out so early every day that I didn't even know what my babies were eating for breakfast, and even though I made my own hours, they still got out of school too early for me to pick them up everyday. Plus, my little one would spend all day with the nanny. This was precious TIME that I wasn't watching them grow and just being with them. Most days looked like: get home, bathe them, feed them, and put them to bed (and sometimes they were already bathed and fed so I had less than an hour with them before their bedtime).

Those first three years of my daughters' lives were a little stressful, trying to juggle two babies and both of us having full-time work, however, I always made the time to exercise and tried to eat well. Nevertheless, I was finding it very difficult to shed my last 15 lbs. after babies. Until one day when a trainer friend of mine walked into the gym looking better than ever, and I asked her what had changed? I had known her for about 15 years and hadn't seen her in a while, yet she looked better than ever at almost 50 years old and was glowing. She mentioned it was the cellular cleansing products that she was on that had transformed her already-fit figure. That was all I needed to hear! This lady was a trusted trainer to celebrities and athletes, and I had always respected her opinion.

Two weeks into the program, I was eating more of the foods I loved and was down 11 lbs! Fast forward two more weeks and I had melted a total of 20 lbs. I was HOOKED! I didn't know much about the products, except that they were all natural and exceeded USDA standards of organic, but I felt the difference in everything from my energy, sleep, mood, overall well-being, and muscle—yes, I now had six-pack abs, real ones! I couldn't shut up about my body being lit up from the inside with my newfound missing link to looking and feeling amazing, and I started to share organically with friends and family. I was doing this with no business focus and I just wanted others to feel the way I was feeling.

One day, my trainer friend called me and invited me to go to a company event. I remember laughing at the thought of being a salesperson (what I thought network marketing was all about) and changing careers. I mean, I had worked eight years to obtain my CPA title and now had 20 years of accounting experience.... I wasn't looking for another profession. Plus, as a corporate accountant, you don't deal with many people, so I lacked people skills and was horrible at sales! I thought, "What would someone like me gain from an event like that?" But, she did pull on my heart strings a bit and mentioned the term "time freedom," and it got me thinking about that painful day I missed my daughter's ballet recital because of work. There was a voice inside me that I couldn't ignore, and I decided, just a couple days before, to fly to Phoenix (across the US for me in Miami) and attend that event. I didn't know it then, but this one decision would completely change my life.

At first, I started to regret my decision of leaving my babies for a couple days. I mean, I barely had time for them as it was and, to make matters worse, I would be gone for my older daughter's first day of school in a new school! But, I reminded myself that I was doing this for THEM and thought of the bigger picture. On the second day of that event, I had an enlightening moment (I like to call it my A-HA!) and I realized that I would never have to miss one single event of my daughters' lives, ever again.

I got home and got to work! It wasn't easy to learn a new profession even though it was a simple business, and life truly tested me along the way. It was heart-breaking to lose who I thought was my best friend at the time because she didn't want to hear me out or support me, yet she joined another competitive company in the exact same industry after years of friendship. My husband didn't support me at first, and his friends would send him hurtful messages about me and what I was doing. And what's worse, he didn't defend me. Heck, many friends from high school were "laughing at me" (those words from a good friend, verbatim). But, I was so very focused on my mission to help others look and feel how I was feeling that I put my blinders on and tried not to take things personally.

I started to receive heart-warming messages from people who I had coached, and that really solidified my belief in the products and the amazing company I was starting to get to know. I began to work on myself, read books, listen to podcasts, and truly started to make my business about others' success before my own. And when my excitement would start to dwindle because of all the obstacles that are normal to this business, I just focused on all the success stories of the people I was helping physically and financially and kept going. There were so many times it got really difficult and I wanted to quit: like when a friend accused me of acting without integrity because she didn't understand the business when my intention the entire time was to do what benefited her above all else, or when another great friend stopped inviting my children to her children's birthday parties because she thought what I was doing was some kind of scheme. So many people misunderstood this business in the beginning, but my belief in the products that had changed my life kept me going, and the more people I would impact, the more bullet-proof I became. I knew I chose to do the right thing in every instance, and I was making a difference, despite the naysayers.

Two months after that first company event I attended, with grit, perseverance, a strong work ethic and on a mission to serve others, I was able to replace my weekly CFO salary and walk away from my career. A year and a half later, I had quadrupled my prior earnings, allowing my husband to walk away from a strong six-figure income to join me. Retiring from corporate America and working our business together strengthened our relationship, eliminated common life stresses, and allowed us the time freedom we had dreamed about, to be very present parents to our young daughters. I humbly share that less than four years after that first company event, we were recognized as the company's 131st millionaires, and our business has kept growing every year as we train others to do what we did!

We now live a life by our own design, without time or money obstacles, where we can work when and from where we want, in our flip-flops and yoga pants. We get to follow our passion to travel as often as we like and have already taken our kids around the world three times during their entire summer vacation instead of putting them in summer camp for three months. Not only have we built a strong financial wall around our girls, but we also recently bought our dream home in our dream neighborhood. And this has all been possible because of my belief in life-changing products, my open-mind to a misunderstood industry, my partnering with a company that aligned with my values, and my not letting disappointment, failure, and a temporary lack of social esteem, deviate me from my mission to show people, especially moms and dads, what's possible. Life in yoga pants has proven to be so much sweeter!

TWEETABLE
"Dream Big. If it offends someone, So what? Dream Bigger!" #LiveFree

Laura Hernandez is a mom of two young girls. She and her husband walked away from successful corporate careers, exponentially exceeding their income, to create a life of choice, time, and financial freedom. Isagenix has recognized them with over 25 awards including being named the company's 131st millionaires. They strive to help others do the same because they feel everyone deserves to be healthy and happy with unlimited resources to travel and be with family.

Lauracpa@hotmail.com
#TeamLiveFree
Facebook: /laura.hernandez.7165

CHAPTER 4

#BossMomma From Welfare to Wealth

by Rachell Brinkerhoff

As the saying goes, it's about the journey not the destination. We are continually growing and evolving. Each of our paths are different but beautiful in their own right. This is my story. Although it isn't finished, it recounts where I began and where I now stand. I hope to inspire the dreamer inside of you. Some of my words may be hard to hear. I share them not for sympathy, but to stand alongside you in spirit and whisper to that dreamer, whatever you need to succeed in life already resides within.

There I was, sitting on the subfloor of our old, rundown, was-to-be dream house in the middle of the jungle in Hawaii, crying and trying to recover from being smacked to the floor by the man who was supposed to love and cherish me till death do us part. I began contemplating what I was doing with my life. I felt disconnected from my soul purpose and had been unhappily married for the past ten years dealing with physical, mental, and emotional abuse. I was riddled with worry and guilt for the future of our two young children who are my world and would become the driving force in creating a new reality I had been yearning for.

It was in this moment I realized I had to take responsibility for my situation and began taking massive action to propel me towards my dreams. I didn't have a degree and some minimum wage job wasn't going to cut it. We were living in the most expensive place in America and an ocean away from family. We loved living in Hawaii and desperately wanted to make it work. I knew I had to start a business! I called my best friend to ask her advice, and it just so happened that she was in the process of starting a wellness business of her own with the largest network marketing company in essential oils. I had no experience with this business model, just a few pre-conceived notions. What I did have was a passion for the essential oils. I knew this was a heart-centered company leading the industry standard in sourcing and providing the highest-quality essential oils available.

My best friend asked me to join her. I took this as a sign. I had already been using the essential oils for the past year, and had countless episodes confirming I was on the right path. My son used to suffer from recurrent ear trouble that only antibiotics would provide temporary relief from. We tried everything for this ongoing problem, and I felt so frustrated as a mother. When I started using essential oils, my son experienced long-term results from the discomfort he'd endured, and I never had to give him another antibiotic again. This was life changing! Essential oils would become our easy go-to for any common health concern and transformed the way I cared for my family.

The business was in total alignment with my soul purpose, teaching people about health and wellness in a conscious way of living. I had been nurturing these foundations in my children since birth. I wanted to be part of this opportunity in every way.

"The greatest medicine of all is teaching people how not to need it." Hippocrates

Lucky for me, my friend was willing to support me in the beginning stages of starting my wellness business. She helped me teach my first classes and thankfully so. My lifelong fear of public speaking was debilitating, and I wasn't sure I could teach on my own.

I had an idea to have a launch party to connect with my community. I wanted to empower others like I was empowered. It took pushing myself out of my comfort zone by making connections with new faces and names. I knew this was the only way to generate the momentum I needed to create my new reality. Not many recruitments happened at the event, but what I learned through the process is, our interactions and connections are like seeds. We sow, we water, and when the season is right, we gather our harvest.

A month after the launch, my marriage hit an all-time low. The abuse increased, and knowledge of some particular events made my heart sink deeper than ever before. The time was now. My husband left town on business, and I took the opportunity to get out of dodge! I reached out to one of my closest friends and humbly explained my situation. She graciously offered my children and I a place to stay until we could get on our feet. I packed the only suitcase we had with what clothes we could fit for the three of us and left our little shack in the jungle with only $20 to our name. We shared a twin bed in her house for a month. Within that time, I filed for divorce, got on welfare, and in addition to my wellness business, I started cleaning vacation rentals seven days a week. This helped to generate the income needed to cover our short-term needs.

At this point my wellness business was just starting out, generating around $300 a month income. As much as I would have loved to have my best friend by my side teaching every class with me, this was not the reality. She lived in Las Vegas and had her own business to run. I needed to step up to the plate and take full ownership of the business I was creating, and I did. It took digging deep within to find courage to show up and teach at events despite my fears of public speaking. I had to find new ways to connect with people and overcome limiting belief systems so that I could follow up with those I had planted seeds with. Nothing worth it comes easy. I threw myself into the fire, which looking back, was the best way to learn how to stand on my own two feet. Often, I prayed no-one would show up to my events so I could avoid the anxiety of standing in front of a room full of eyes staring back at me. Sometimes that prayer was answered. Having an empty room can be quite discouraging especially when I invested so much time and effort with high expectations, even if it helped me avoid the anxiety. I did not allow this to stop me. I knew the only way to achieve my goal of being a stay-at-home mom again and providing our dream life, would come by way of consistency in teaching weekly events, following up, and training and supporting my growing team. I kept this vision that was dear to my heart at the forefront of every decision I faced.

I knew short-term sacrifices needed to be made so I could participate in the long-term payoffs. I found a run-down, 500 square foot, one bedroom apartment for $850 a month. It was barely in my budget, but a score to find! My kids and I would continue to share a bed over the next five months. I would borrow pots and pans from my neighbor just to cook on, and at times forgo paying the electric bill to make ends meet. This was the most emotionally challenging time of my life. With no personal space or time and hardly a pot to piss in, we were barely scraping by when news came we had to move. Every rental was $1,000 plus, and most only allowed for one tenant. I could barely afford the cardboard box I was currently renting and had no idea what the future held.

One evening I was walking around the block with a friend, sharing my situation. We turned a corner and came upon a "For Rent" sign. A gleam of hope shot through my heart. I inquired about the rental from the man mowing the lawn. He happened to be the owner. He walked us through the cottage. It wasn't much bigger than my current apartment, but it had two bedrooms, and I fell in love!

Then I found out that this new cottage was $1500 a month plus deposit. In that moment, I told myself that I could afford it! I filled out the application and handed it to the man. I was determined to get the cottage! I had begun envisioning myself living there, the furniture I would have to decorate it, my kids running through the house and playing in the yard. I was really feeling the emotions of how it would be to live there with my family.

Though I did not have the $3,000 to get the cottage, I did have the faith of a mustard seed. I was incredibly close to achieving a leadership rank with the network marketing company that paid exactly $1,500 a month.

The cottage wasn't going to be available to move in for another month, and I still had a month left on my current lease. This bought me some time to work extra hard to make it happen! The cottage wasn't a guarantee, nor was hitting rank, but I had the "faith it till you make it" attitude, put my trust into the universe, and took action.

My hard work paid off, and I achieved that leadership rank (just six months into my career). I got the phone call that I was the right fit for the cottage despite the 100s of offers they'd received. My car got hit in a parking lot right in front of me, imparting only cosmetic damages, and a couple weeks later I received a check from their insurance company in the exact amount of $1,500, just in time to move. With $3,000 in my hand, I left my cardboard box, upgraded to the cutest beach cottage in the neighborhood, and my belief system deepened.

A year later, I hit the next leadership rank in the company and completely replaced the income from my cleaning business. The timing couldn't have been better. Being a maid wasn't my soul calling, though I was very grateful for it and all it provided for us during that phase in our life. I found a reliable replacement and quit my day job!

I became a full-time professional network marketer! That's when my wellness business really took off, and I could step into a leadership role that would take my team to the next level. From then on, my team continued to grow. I maintained rank and began to enjoy public speaking. I could now afford to stay at home with my children and support them in the way I had been dreaming of, even taking them traveling across the country with me to support my growing teams in other states, helping those team members get started, just like my best friend had done for me.

Three years into building my wellness business, I achieved the second highest paying rank in the company, turning what was a three-figure income into a six-figure income. We've since moved from our beloved beach cottage into our dream home on the beach that, funny enough, I used to clean. I call this "a high attraction lifestyle." Fast forward five years later, I am currently one of the top income earners in the company and well on my way to earning the number one paid rank.

If I could turn back the hands of time and impart wisdom to myself as I was starting my business it would be this: Do not compare yourself to anyone. YOU ARE ENOUGH! Your journey is special unto you. You were created with your own set of unique talents and gifts that nobody else possesses and you need to share them with the world your way. This does not mean you need to reinvent the wheel, just do things with your own style. Stumbling blocks are only stumbling blocks if we let them hold us back instead of allowing an opportunity to learn, grow, and overcome. By choosing to find a way to make it work, you will not only gain wisdom and knowledge, you will also train your mind to find avenues of success in any area of your life.

The beauty in this is the power to not only change your life, but also the lives lucky enough to be touched by yours. And finally, don't skimp on investing in yourself! Personal development is the key. Be willing to be brutally honest with who you are. Identify skills you don't have that you'll need to develop in order to become the best version of you! This is what creates a high attraction lifestyle that will allow you to attract dynamic and influential people into your life and your business. Continue to evaluate your inner circle and live by the 90-10 rule. Spend 90% of your time with people who inspire you, who you can learn from, people who love and celebrate you and all of your awesomeness. Spend the other 10% of your time providing all this goodness for someone else who needs it. Most importantly, lead with your heart and be on a mission to serve.

I want to express my deepest thanks and gratitude for my beautiful North Shore community who have been part of our journey and have loved and supported us along the way. Thank you to all my friends and family for being such a solid support system when I was feeling weak and wanting to give up. Your belief in me and words of encouragement kept me going.

I'd like to invite you to take a chance and follow your dreams. Not tomorrow, not next week, but today! Every second matters, and you have one opportunity at this life to make it the best you've ever had. YOU ARE WORTH IT!

TWEETABLE
"Our connections are like seeds. We sow, we water, and when the time is right, we gather our harvest."

Rachell Brinkerhoff is a ground-breaking entrepreneur, powerhouse mamma of two, heart-centered humanitarian, mentor, and an expert on essential oils and conscious living. From humble beginnings and now a passionate wellness warrior— Rachell is a six-figure income earner, holds Blue Diamond Leadership in DoTERRA, and mentors 30,000+ people with a monthly, growing network of 1500+.

To ignite your wellness wishes, connect with Rachell here:
rachell@essentialsforliving.earth
Instagram: essentialsfor_living
Facebook: https://www.facebook.com/ essentialforliving/
www.mydoterra.com/theessentialsforliving

CHAPTER 5

From My Parents' Basement to Two Grammys

by Seth Mosley

grew up in a small town called Circleville, Ohio. You've never heard of it. It is a small dot on a map 40 miles south of Columbus. And it's claim to fame is not music. It's...wait for it...

PUMPKINS! Our town is so proud of their pumpkins that they even built a water tower that looks like a pumpkin and host a week long pumpkin extravaganza every year called The Pumpkin Show. Heck, my parents were so proud of it, they even entered me in the pumpkin baby parade! So I hope you're getting the point that I wasn't born in Music City, USA.

My first exposure to music was in church. When I couldn't even walk yet, my parents would take me to their choir rehearsals and let me sit on their lap, and I'd memorize all of the songs before I could put sentences together. As I grew up, my dad (who wasn't really all that musical) would take me to concerts and buy me CDs. My first CD was from a band called Newsboys. You'll find out later why this is worth noting. Music was a constant part of my development, and I started to learn piano and guitar, probably having a total of about five lessons, but teaching myself instead. I eventually started leading on stage at church when I got into my teenage years. The only reason I ended up on stage was because there was no one else. I helped out with my youth group a ton, saw a need, had a passion, and raised my hand. I had never actually sang in front of anyone before, and being on stage was actually quite nerve-racking. But it was the way I felt like I could serve.

Eventually, I figured out a way to start recording myself and my really bad songs on my parents' computer at home. I eventually saved up enough money to buy some basic gear and start a recording studio in our basement. I was HOOKED. I would only come up for air, food, and water. And that was where I found my calling as a music producer and songwriter. I learned the art of this creative process by doing it over and over again, really badly, I might add. Then, one day I finished a song that I felt like wasn't totally embarrassing and uploaded it to the internet. I put my work out there. And I got lots of good feedback from people. I thought maybe I was onto something. And then I did something crazy that would change my life forever.

I had a friend named Mike. He was way cooler than me. He had a band. He played guitar really well. I called him up one day and said, "Hey Mike, guess what? I'm a music producer now and I have this sweet studio," which in reality was a computer and a couple speakers and a few microphones, and it was crazy for me to call myself a music producer. "I want to produce your band's record. And I'll do it for 100 bucks!"

"Ummm...sounds good," he answered.

Profound conversation, I know. Doesn't sound life-changing, I know. But let me tell you why it was.

I produced their five song EP, spent countless days and months slaving away over every detail of the sound. And by the way, I didn't know what I was doing. I had never done this before with anyone else's music. So I was learning how to actually produce as we went. When we all finally decided it was great, we put it out there. And it was a hit. At least two dozen copies sold. But then, my phone rang one day, and I remember exactly where I was sitting, in my dad's office at home. I picked up, "Hello?"

"Hi, my name is Carl, and I have a recording studio up in Columbus. I heard this record you did. You are doing some great stuff." It took me a minute to figure out, "Does he have the wrong number? Oh, THAT record that we just did in my parents' basement!"

"I'm expanding my production business and need someone to take over creative," he said.

"Would you like to come and work for me and produce full-time?" Meanwhile, on the other end of the line, I was internally freaking out. I was enrolled to go to college for music business, probably to learn how to be a producer anyway, and here this guy was offering me a full-time job to start doing it RIGHT AWAY!

So, like any smart person, I said "Yes" and started working two weeks later. I was doing the job that I was going to go to college to hopefully get. And I was getting paid for it! I would have paid the guy for the experience, let alone make a full-time salary. And working for him was where I got my 10,000 hours. I didn't care what I was doing. Some days I was producing bands and other days I was learning how to solder headphone cables together. It was all a blast! I was just pumped to be in the environment, and the best thing I could do was to serve any way possible. I learned 10x more by going in saying, "How can I serve?" rather than "How can I impress someone?"

This was a whirlwind year and a half. I loved it but had an itch inside to do my own thing. So I started my own band, trying to be as cool as my friend, Mike! And like anything else I do in life, I threw myself into it completely. I set up something like a telemarketing center, again in my parents' basement, and we made 50-100 phone calls a day offering to come and play at different venues across the country. Most people said no. But if we got one yes for the day, you'd better believe we were doing backflips! We ended up filling up a whole tour and then 150 shows for three solid years. We even ended up going all the way across the ocean to Sweden and played my favorite show in my entire touring career. Why? Because it was at that show that I met my wife.

We instantly knew. There was no question in my mind. She had never been to our country, and didn't even have a passport. But this didn't matter because it was meant to be. We got married exactly a year later and got our first house together in Nashville, TN—Music City, USA.

I should mention that I never made any money at the band. I was producing records for artists on the side to keep the band afloat. It eventually got to be so much of a burden because I was trying to be three things at once—a husband, a songwriter, and an artist. I learned the hard way from this season: IF YOU CHASE TWO RABBITS, YOU CATCH NEITHER. I was lacking the one key thing I needed to achieve success at any of them, FOCUS.

F - FIERCE

O - OBSESSIVE

C - CONCENTRATED

U - UNRELENTING

S - SACRIFICE

You probably know by now which path I chose. I took off the artist hat and decided to spend all my time at home becoming the best music producer and songwriter that I could be. I started a company called Full Circle Music because of this.

Remember how I told you my first CD I got when I was a kid was Newsboys? Well, the first major label project I was hired to produce in Nashville was, you guessed it—Newsboys. It was a record called "Born Again." Talk about a full circle moment. I wore their records out as a kid growing up and here I was getting to press record and help bring to life a record for this same band that I loved so much. Mind you, I had never produced a label project before. I felt like I was still winging it. But the one thing I knew how to do was to serve. So I looked for any way to do that possible. Sometimes that meant producing their music, and sometimes that meant driving them in a car down down to Atlanta and back for a meeting. Just like my time in the studio in Columbus, it didn't matter what I was doing. I was just immersed in music and loving every second.

Needless to say, the sky has been the limit for Full Circle Music since then. We have won two Grammy Awards, four Dove Awards, Billboard's #1 Producer of the Year in 2013, and SESAC #1 Songwriter of the Year in 2014. We have had 22 #1 radio singles and been a part of countless Gold and Platinum records sold worldwide. Our songs have been in major Hollywood films and TV commercials. And guess what our number one company core value is? SERVANTHOOD.

My hope is that my story and my success can remind you that if I can do it, anyone can do it. I was not born in LA or Nashville. I didn't come from a musically successful family. I barely have any formal music training. I have no college degree. And I saw my first #1 when I was 22, and I'm 28 now, so it really isn't even about age.

It isn't even about who is the most trained, qualified, or resourced. It is about who has the most drive, passion, and stick-to-it-iveness. But most of all, it is about being a servant. None of my success in life has been because I am the most gifted person in the room. In fact, it's been the opposite. I've had to serve, because I've been in over my head every season of my life. I've been in rooms and sat at tables I didn't deserve to sit at; I hadn't earned any right to. But what goes a lot further than trying to be impressive, is to look at who is sitting across from you in the room and asking, "How can I serve this person right now?" Sometimes for me, it has nothing to do with music. But that's ok. Because at the end of the day, music is what I do. It isn't who I am. Who I am is a servant. And though it sounds completely counter-intuitive, being a servant brings the greatest satisfaction out of anything you can do in life. Money gets old and goes away. Cars lose their novelty. Exotic vacations get boring. #1s fall off the chart. But serving others, now that's something that we all have deeply ingrained in us as humans. Becoming a servant is the highest thing in life we can achieve.

This idea of servanthood is what inspired me to start Full Circle Academy. We are on a mission to change the music industry from the inside out, by finding and empowering the next generation of producers, songwriters, and artists to make music at the highest possible level. If we have anything to do with it, this next generation won't be famous because they are rock stars, but they will be famous because they are serving this world like it has never been served before. Music has power. It changes lives, and even saves them sometimes. We want to be a part of speaking life into anyone trying to make it in the music business, and to give them a place to learn how.

Full Circle Academy is doing this by providing education and mentorship through real-world hands-on experience and virtual coaching.

As a husband and a father of a beautiful daughter and another on the way, I am especially blessed to have a world-class recording studio in our house. People come to me. I get to spend time with my family starting in the morning and as soon as sessions are finished. I'm intentional to put my family and spiritual life first.

I'm honored to share my story in this book. I never dreamed I would have a platform to share my philosophy and ideas outside the music world. In fact, in 2016 Kyle Wilson pushed me way outside my comfort zone when he ask me to speak and share my story at his 3-day Weekend Event with Brian Tracy, Darren Hardy, and other professional speakers.

I've learned to always answer the calls from your mentors and the people in your life with a yes. Good things are always on the other side.

TWEETABLE
It sounds completely counter-intuitive, but becoming a servant is the highest thing in life we can achieve. #fullcirclemusic

Seth Mosley, at only the age of 29, is a two-time GRAMMY award winning producer, the 2013 Billboard Magazine #1 Christian Music Producer of the Year and #3 Christian Songwriter, 2014 SESAC Christian Songwriter of the Year, and the writer of 28 charting radio singles. He is the Lessons From Network Music Contributor and has written over 600 songs. Seth's recent production credits include: Michael W. Smith, TobyMac, for KING & COUNTRY, Unspoken, Jeremy Camp, Sidewalk Prophets, Audio Adrenaline, Blanca, Moriah Peters, and Jared Anderson. Seth Mosley is the Founder of Full Circle Music.

www.fullcirclemusic.org
info@fullcirclemusic.org
Instagram: fullcirclemusicco

CHAPTER 6

The Birth of a New Family

by Mark and Tamiel Kenney

"*A*chieving a dream is about more than what you accomplish. It's about who you become in the process!" — JOHN MAXWELL

I was 20 and Mark 23 when we were married in 1995. We were young and full of hope of what our future life together would be like. We learned the value of hard work as we both came from families of very modest incomes. We knew we did not want to struggle financially like our parents did and looked for ways to make additional income. So, we started buying smaller multifamily apartments that we managed and fixed up in our not-so-spare time. This was on top of Mark's very demanding IT job, where he constantly traveled, and my job in healthcare. We both agreed we loved real estate but did not enjoy being landlords, and we also agreed we did not plan on working corporate jobs for the next 30-40 years for someone else, on their terms. So in 2008, Mark started his own IT company and did very well consulting for companies such as T-Mobile, Marathon Oil, Northrop Grumman, and Lockheed Martin. However, he neglected his first love, which was real estate.

In 2013, we made a bold and somewhat scary decision to give up our high-paying income and follow our dream of becoming full-time real estate investors. It was certainly challenging, but today, Mark and I work full-time together investing in real estate. We own over 1700 multifamily apartment units, hold educational seminars, and mentor others interested in multifamily apartment investing. Our road to success has been, and continues to be, filled with obstacles to climb and fires to walk through to get where we are now. I don't know how we made it through some days, but we are much stronger because of the trials we have overcome. Today, we are both completely different people than when we started.

"Communication is the lifeline of any relationship. Without it, the relationship will starve itself to death." Elizabeth Bourrgeret

One area where we have experienced significant growth is the way we communicate with each other and others. Mark and I did not communicate very well with each other for many years, which caused significant struggles within our marriage. He will admit that part of it was his ego, and the other part was my desire to run away from conflict, which made communicating effectively nearly impossible. This caused a number of issues in our relationship, and it took some drastic events in our marriage to force a shift in our thinking. Trials are painful at the time, but necessary for growth. This holds true for growing a business as well as growing relationships. After 21 years of marriage, we have finally learned the art of communication with the help of a marriage counselor. The exciting news is our marriage is stronger now than it has ever been. We have also been able to take these same communication lessons learned and apply them to our business. We have learned to be active listeners, as the best communicators are also the best listeners.

"I haven't failed. I just found 10,000 ways that didn't work." —THOMAS EDISON

We have tried many business adventures to gain financial freedom and gotten excited about what could be, only to be disappointed when it did not go as planned. One hard lesson we learned was when Mark was working IT consulting. He started working with a guy that he trusted at first but found out that he was not paying some of the other consultants. However, he continued to pay Mark and compliment him as well as make promises such as having Mark take over the company in a couple years. So, Mark continued to work with him even though he knew his employer could not be trusted, and he did not treat people with respect the way Mark would treat them. Why? His actions did not directly affect us and because of the potential for future income. Mark naively trusted the lies he was told. Then, before we knew it, Mark stopped being paid and was owed more than $150,000. We had to live off our credit cards at this time as we had already worked through our savings while we were waiting for him to stay true to his word. We felt embarrassed and, quite frankly, stupid for letting this get out of hand. The main lesson we learned is when your gut tells you something is not right, even if you are not impacted personally, take action, and don't stay in the situation. A person's true character will always come through, especially when money is involved. Have the courage and wisdom to cut your losses and move on!

"Miracles start to happen when you give as much energy to your dreams as you do to your fears." —RICHARD WILKINS

As Mark and I worked through our communication issues, we also worked together on creating a strong legacy of financial freedom for our children (Tyler, 12 and Paige, 9) by investing in apartments. While we planned to continue to work less as we built our real estate portfolio, life propelled us in another direction. We started to face changes with the people we were in a professional community with. We observed things happening that we did not agree with from an ethical standpoint, and we decided to disassociate from this group. This decision could have significantly impacted our business for the worse. But, instead of allowing fear to paralyze us, we had faith that we would still achieve our dreams. Once we left that community, people started reaching out to us on a daily basis. All of them were looking to be a part of a community where they felt valued. A shift happened for us at this moment. We were determined to create our own community, our own family, and our company. Think Multifamily was born.

"When you know you're right, you're not afraid of fighting back." —ROBERT KIYOSAKI

Even though starting our own community is not what we had planned, we have both found our passion. We couldn't be more excited about the opportunity to work together as a team, serving others in our community. We have had a blast building relationships within our business that have turned into lifelong friendships. We discovered that we both really enjoy hosting training events for our community and giving back what we have learned over the years.

However, we have also experienced some trials. As entrepreneurs, we face challenges on a regular basis; it is how you respond to those challenges that determines your future. Our most recent challenge is facing a modern day bully who leads by fear and intimidation. The world is full of bullies. I was bullied as a teen, and now Mark and I are facing a bully as adults. Fear and intimidation may work on some, but for those who are confident in their purpose, in their calling, there is no greater force that propels us to stand up for what is right! Years ago I would have been lead by fear. Now I choose to stand up and fight. As we hold true to our values, always do what is right even when no one is looking, and stand for what is right even if we stand alone, we continue to build our community with others who also share these same values.

"Formal education will make you a living; self-education will make you a fortune." —JIM ROHN

As we continue to build our dreams and help others pursue theirs, we wanted to make sure we also teach our children to build their own dreams and not someone else's. Mark and I felt the best way to teach our children the life of entrepreneurship was to homeschool them full-time and include them in our business. We are able to supplement our children's schoolwork with real world education. Tyler and Paige assist with the setup of our events and talk with guests as they arrive; Paige assists with the registration of guests, and they both kick off the event with an introduction of our family. We even have Tyler looking at analyzing real estate deals on a simple application developed by Mark. Homeschooling also has been a blessing for our family as the kids are now able to observe us in our business as we work from home, as well as assist us with our training events. We believe this benefits our family as well as others who may have the same desire to make family entrepreneurship a way of life. Our future goal is to create an entrepreneurship program for teens, to help open their eyes to possibilities *they never imagined.*

"Never believe that a few caring people can't change the world. For, indeed, that's all who ever has." —Margaret Mead

As our Think Multifamily family continues to grow, we hope to set the example for our community in their pursuit of creating a legacy for themselves and their families. As you continue to follow your dreams, we hope that you will take courage to overcome obstacles, communicate honestly, learn from your failures, push past your fears, and stand up for what is right. Being a mom and dadpreneur is a blessing. We encourage you to find a way every day to be a blessing to others!

TWEETABLE
"Formal education will make you a living; self-education will make you a fortune." —Jim Rohn
#Legacy #Community #Thinkmultifamily

Mark and Tamiel Kenney are full-time real estate investors, educators, entrepreneurs, and founders of Think Multifamily. They have a passion to help others wisely invest in real estate. Tamiel is a published author and was previously an RN and executive admin. Mark was previously a CPA and IT consultant. They have two wonderful children, Tyler and Paige.

Mark, in addition to creating tech apps, enjoys UFC, cars, and funny movies. Tamiel enjoys reading, music, and missions.

Facebook: Think Multifamily
Tami@thinkmultifamily.com
thinkmultifamily.com

CHAPTER 7

#BucketListGoalCrusher

by Dawn Cermak

"Thank you for being my inspiration to do crazy things like move to the opposite side of the world. You make fulfilling your dreams look easy!!! I can't wait for you to come visit me so you can cross another place off your bucket list!!!"

This is the note my 22-year-old daughter Lucy wrote and left for me to find after heading off to teach English in Thailand. At the very moment I read that, I knew in my heart that I had succeeded in one of my main goals as a parent. Because, clearly, she truly BELIEVES she can do anything she sets her mind to! She truly BELIEVES that living the life of her dreams is possible! She BELIEVES she deserves and is ready to go out and grab everything that life has to offer!

Have I always made it look easy? Heck no! I have been an entrepreneur for 28 years. When I was pregnant with my first son, my husband and I knew we wanted me to stay home with our children. So, I started a database management company. Shortly thereafter, I started a special events company with my sister. My husband had the "real job," and he supported us while I worked on growing those two companies.

Eleven years later, I had moved my focus from the database company, and the special events company we started had become wildly successful! We had grown the company to annual sales of 8 million and 140 employees! It was very rewarding to be so successful. We had moved to a beautiful home in an excellent school district, the kids' college accounts were significantly funded, and we had gone on some great vacations and had nice cars. However, it had come at a huge cost. I wasn't able to spend time with my kids and husband and really be present with them in their lives.

December was not a time of Christmas cookie baking, decorating the tree, and going to see The Nutcracker ballet, it was a time when I was out doing big holiday parties for companies like AOL.

Weekends were not family time—that is when all the big events were! And even when I was "off," the phone would ring, and I would have to drop everything, leave my kids' games and swim meets, leave their playdates, and leave family parties to handle the "emergency." Every single vacation we took had to be scheduled around payroll. In fact, the morning after I had my third child, my sister showed up with a giant vase filled with 50 pink roses…and the payroll packet. I sent my daughter back to the nursery so I could sign all the checks and thought, "there must be a better way." I knew I had to figure it out.

And so I did. I told my sister I needed to focus on my family. She agreed, and we put the company up for sale. It was one of the best decisions we ever made! The company sold, and I was able to take a step back while we transitioned in the new ownership. Working "part-time," and having someone else carry the heavy responsibility of operating the company was such a relief! We began renovating an old farm house, had a fourth child, and took some fun vacations. Life was good! Except for one thing. It turned out I was not very good at not being in charge. I was not very good at taking direction from others. I was not very good at accepting and executing someone else's vision.

Finally, with the new ownership firmly in place, we left the company and looked forward. I was determined to learn from my mistakes. I was determined to design my life to put my family first. I was determined to be in control of my time. I was determined to find something that would fulfill my desire to be of service and support and empower other entrepreneurs.

We called it our Golden Summer. We finally had time to focus on family fun and time to focus on our own health and fitness. My sister "tasked" me with finding a nutritional system to support our efforts. And I found it! Nutritional products and a system that produced amazing results, or your money back! What did we have to lose…besides some pounds and inches? We used the system and lost the pounds and inches. Our energy went through the roof, and we were seeing the results of our workouts at the gym.

Initially, I had no idea that there was a business opportunity with the company. At that time, I had some pretty strong assumptions and beliefs about network marketing and ZERO interest in direct sales. After all, I had no sales skills. My experience was in building and running companies! However, when I studied this company's unique and powerful compensation plan and I realized that not only could I create income and time freedom for myself, but I could also create it for members of my family, I knew I had to at least give it a try, even though I knew very little about nutrition and supplements and NOTHING about network marketing!

I set out to create a business model for doing this "network marketing thing" because the home party model was not a fit for me. Nor was "harassing my friends and family." I did start to build a team, slowly but consistently. And I LOVED the time freedom! I LOVED being at the school bus stop every day, being at all of the boys' sporting events, working when my kids were at school and being there when they got home to hear about their day. I LOVED having Mommy-Mayzie days every Thursday, and being able to take vacations and not worry about payroll!

Meanwhile, my sister, brother, and I had started a new event company. We agreed that they would run that company, and I would continue to work with my health and wellness team. The event company experienced explosive growth and we re-acquired the company we had sold. I jumped in to help with the merger and acquisition and to consolidate the two companies. It was intense! It did not take long to remember all of the things I did not like about having to go to an office every day and not having control of my time. It was not a happy time for me. My husband and I divorced. I knew it was time to again reevaluate my priorities and make some serious changes.

I had always dreamed of moving to another country, learning the language, and completely immersing in the culture and community. In 2014 I scooped up my eight-year-old and off we went to live in Barcelona. She attended the International School of Barcelona, I was a member of the Barcelona Entrepreneurs Organization, and we both met people from all over the world. Even though it was just the two of us, we rented a big house and invited all of our friends and family to come and share our Mediterranean lifestyle with us!

While we were there, my older daughter came for the summer, and we traveled all over—Brussels, Paris, Amsterdam, Valencia, Madrid, wherever we wanted! My sister, Robin, also joined me in Barcelona. We worked our global business together, sitting at seaside cafes, really and truly living the dream. It was truly the adventure of a lifetime. I believe that is when the #BucketListGoalCrusher was born. And the best part was, I still got paid by my health and wellness company every Monday! Because, even though I was living abroad, I was still able to work my business, thanks to modern technology, and was earning residual income.

Upon our return from Barcelona, in the fall of 2014, we decided to really dive in and take our business to the next level. Two years later, I became millionaire #205 with our company, and my sister is right behind me!

I am a huge believer in the power and importance of recognition: recognition of goals achieved, small and large, and recognition of people out doing good in the world. I was constantly buying and sending small things to recognize the accomplishments of my team members, spending hours and hours searching for inspirational jewelry and cards, and then running to the post office to mail them out. Realizing that others were probably frustrated and wasting valuable time doing the same, I created a site for inspirational gifts. Now recognition is a click of a button!

It is said that network marketing is personal growth with a compensation plan attached. I believe my strong commitment to personal growth, for myself and for those on my team, has been a significant factor in our success. I have attended and also staffed numerous personal growth and leadership seminars over the years. I am passionate about continuing to grow and supporting others on their journey. So passionate, in fact, that I am working on a concept for an international personal growth seminar series, as well as an international immersion and exchange program…stay tuned!

I think the true key to our success is that we have a system that can be duplicated. We have a strong support network of proven, committed coaches…and I have a magic whiteboard! When I talk to a new team member, I ask them about their goals and dreams. We both get very clear on their vision, and then we create an individualized roadmap for turning those dreams into reality. I tell them they do not have to understand every aspect of this compensation plan to get started, because I understand it and know how to maximize it, and I will teach them along the way! Just get into ACTION! And then I put their name and their dreams on my magic whiteboard. What is magic about it? The dreams come true!

I am writing this chapter on a plane coming home from London where I have just been house hunting. Our company is getting ready to launch in the European market, and I intend to be an integral part of it! Finding a six bedroom house in London, one with a piano (because learning how to play the piano is on my bucket list) was no small feat, but I need one that big. My daughters will be coming for the summer. I'm hoping my sons can come too (however, right now their accelerating careers are their priority), and I will be hosting my team members who want to join me as I and start building an international team!

"The biggest adventure you can ever take is to live the life of your dreams." I AM living the life of my dreams…and you can too!

#BucketListGoalCrusher #ICanWorkFromAnywhereInTheWorld #ILoveMyLife

TWEETABLE

Formula for Success: Clear Intention + Discipline + Proven Committed Coach = Explosive Results! #DreamAchieveRepeat!

Dawn Cermak is an International Business and Success Coach, Global Connector, Serial Entrepreneur, Compensation Plan Specialist, Business Strategist, Footloose World Traveler, Charitable Giver, Lover of Languages, Inspirational Gift Buyer, Leader of Leaders/Leader of Self, Personal Growth Aficionado, Philanthropist, Legacy Funder, and Bucket List Goal Crusher!

www.DawnCermak.com
https://www.facebook.com/dawn.cermak.1
Instagram: @Dawn.Cermak
Dawn.Cermak@gmail.com
Health And Wellness: www.dawncermak.isagenix.com
Inspirational Gifts: www.giftstoinspire.us

CHAPTER 8

Claiming My Worth

Becoming a Millionaire Mom on a Mission

by Janine Brolly

I am a born cheerleader for women. I believe I was influenced at a very young age, coming into this world sensing the hardship women incurred from current and past generations, and their tenacity to triumph and rise above it all to create better lives for themselves!

The first six days of my life were spent nestled in the arms of my birth mother, unsure if she was going to keep me or not. She wanted to, but I was a product of a passionate love affair, a circumstance that was considered taboo back in the day. On that sixth day, she gave me up for adoption, and it broke her heart. I later learned that she went on to lead a fulfilling life, ironically marrying my birth father, and had another daughter. She also became a very successful entrepreneur.

At six weeks old, I was adopted into a new, loving family where my mom grew into what I now refer to as my "hero." She was unable to have children of her own due to having tuberculosis and complications when she was 17. She was incredibly loving and gracious and knew how to suck all she could out of life! Later on, her tenaciousness and willingness to fight served her well when she was diagnosed with advanced ovarian cancer and given one year to live. I was lucky to have her for another four years. Then it was time to say goodbye to another mother.

My entrepreneurial and tenacious traits didn't just come from my mothers. Two of my grandmothers experienced great hardship and heartache and yet were able to live happy and fulfilling lives through perseverance and determination to not just survive, but to truly thrive! With all this in my blood and my upbringing (nature and nurture), I was set to live my life as a driven go-getter, but I was going to find out the hard way that there was a missing piece.

Here's where it really started to become apparent that I was headed in a direction that I didn't realize could end in burnout. Let's just say it was a blurry and busy stage of my life: going through a divorce, losing my mom to ovarian cancer, selling our home and moving my two young daughters to a new one, and building a business. Working hard, even pushing myself, was my normal state. I was living on overdrive but it didn't occur to me that it would catch up with me one day.

As a single mother (for 70% of the time) and health professional for 20 years, I had also just left my corporate position as the director of one of the largest health and wellness programs in British Columbia to pursue entrepreneurship full-time in network marketing of all things! Crazy? Yes, to some, I am sure. But entrepreneurship was in my blood, and there was no denying this deep knowing of mine. My biggest driving factor was to create more freedom to live life on my own terms and ultimately have more time with my daughters. I was also driven to be the best role model I could be for my girls!

After an 18-year relationship, my husband and I parted ways. I later dated a wonderful man and we fell in love. However, during our year and a bit together I was seeing how different and incompatible we really were. I broke it off, and I was heartbroken. I certainly didn't want to feel this pain and loss again, and I wondered if there was a common denominator in these relationships.

Then came my epiphany. "Enough!" I said. It's time to take stock of what I needed in order to be able to fully live my purpose. I was putting others' needs before mine, making them more important, relying on external validation to tell me I was okay instead of being connected to myself and my inner resources! This was my M.O. everywhere in my life: my career, my relationships, everywhere! I had created lots of outer success, but I did it with "proving" energy. Proving that I was good enough. I couldn't believe that I had been living most of my life trying to prove my worth!

I think at a deep level I believed I wasn't worthy since my birth mother didn't want me. My unconscious messaging was, if I didn't make others important or make them happy (even if it came at a cost to me), I might be rejected again. In the process, I was literally giving away my energy...and my power! Over time, this depleted me and thus was my pattern of burnout!

I learned there is a difference between giving "of" yourself and giving "up" yourself. It was in this epiphany moment, that I made a declaration to reclaim me! To focus on my showing up for myself, my girls, and my career. I realized the way I do anything is the way I do everything! The only way I could fulfill my calling to truly serve, inspire, and create an impact was if I was in my power, doing this for myself first, with nothing to prove, just owning it! Simply put, I WAS CLAIMING MY WORTH!

This declaration changed everything and truly catapulted me on a personal level as well as my business. I quadrupled my income from my prior corporate position! And of course, my daughters reaped the benefits big time! With greater time and financial freedom, I have been able to work from home, see them off to and home from school, and be at almost ALL their school functions and sports. As well, I have been able to provide incredible experiences for them, including some wonderful mother-daughter trips... absolutely priceless! When my eldest daughter asked if she could go on a "field trip" to Nepal for 30 days with a small group of students from a pool of several high schools, I was able to say "yes" where many families would not have been able to afford it. It turned out to be a life-changing trip that she still talks about to this day! The other blessing was the time I had with my mom in her last four years right up to the final weeks, days, and even breathes of her life. I was fortunate to be alongside her where I was most needed. My mom gifted me with some beautiful experiences in these final moments that forever changed me. I often reflect how my most precious and treasured days of my life were the days that I brought my daughters into the world and the day I was with my mom as she left this world. Again...priceless!

I have since gone on to become a seven-figure earner with my network marketing business. Believe me, grateful doesn't even begin to describe how I feel! So how did this internal shift make such a huge impact in my life and business? Well, I believe that true success is an inside job. Most people, when creating a financial or life goal, focus on what's outside of them (money, appearance, status, purchases, etc). When I turned my focus inwards, connected to my own purpose and truth, and experienced how I wanted to feel, I was able to grasp that I was worthy of a life full of riches far beyond money. When I became aligned with my knowing and created from this pure, potent, and connected place, miracles happened!

And now, through my own journey and having worked with hundreds of women, I realize how epidemic it is that most women do not fully value themselves, and as a result, do not fully show up in the world. Their stories may be different, whether they were influenced by past generations of oppression or conditioned in this lifetime, or both, the limiting beliefs like mine, such as "not feeling worthy" or "not good enough" are universal! I believe it's time we collectively make an internal shift and claim our worth! For me, my wounding at birth, actually birthed my greatest gift: to learn to claim my worth and, in turn, support women to also claim their birthright and fully own their worth.

It is my mission to continue to cheerlead and be an advocate for worthy women, facilitating and empowering women to claim their worth personally, professionally, and financially. I do this through speaking and spreading the message, hosting events, and the Worthy & Wealthy Women's Mastermind. The legacy I am creating also includes philanthropic work for women and girls in developing countries. My dream is for my daughters to be involved with this one day too! I believe I am here to shout from the rooftop, "You don't need permission to be big, bold, or beautiful! You already are! You are valuable and powerful! It's time to claim it for yourself, your children, your community, and for humanity!"

TWEETABLE

Women, you do not need permission to be big, bold or beautiful. You already are. It's your birthright! Claim it!

Janine Brolly is a Speaker, Mentor, Social Entrepreneur, Isagenix Millionaire and Founder of the Worthy & Wealthy Women's Mastermind. She believes most women do not fully value themselves and, as a result, do not fully show up in the world. Janine's mission is to create massive impact, as an advocate, empowering women to **SHOW UP MORE** *in their lives.*

Janine@janinebrolly.com
www.janinebrolly.com
www.powherhouse.com/janine-brolly

CHAPTER 9

Our Journey of Healing, Family, and Hope

by Scott and Susan Wooley

After a miraculous healing from an inoperable brachial plexus nerve tumor, without chemo, radiation, or surgery, we had one prayer. God, allow us to use our testimony to lead, inspire, encourage, and give HOPE to others.

It was 2010. Scott, a real estate veteran with over 700 transactions and north of $80 million in sales, and Susan, a homeschooling mother to three, were about to learn the incredible power of prayer.

We began handcrafting fish tacos and fresh salsa in our kitchen for friends during UFC watch parties. The crowds grew and grew. We've always loved preparing food for our friends. It's how we roll! Many times we would find ourselves around the kitchen connecting instead of in front of the TV. We both realized that FOOD brings people together. FOOD breaks down barriers, and FOOD is a universal language. FOOD feeds people. We wanted to feed HOPE to the people! A taco concept was supernaturally planted in our minds. Maybe we could use food to share our story. We prayed, cooked, and repeated the process. Before long, we had recipes for 3-4 tacos, a couple salsas, guacamole, and a very distinctive flavor profile—a Southern California flavor profile. The name was perfect. So-Cal Tacos was born.

With three kids and one on the way, Scott quit his job, we bought a food truck and pushed our chips in the game. We are now in the HOPE giving business full-time via $3 tacos from a food truck. After months and months of planning, branding, navigating various city codes, and countless hours, the time was near to "deliver" So-Cal Tacos. However, before doing so, we had another "work of art" to introduce first. We welcomed our fourth child in September 2011 and introduced the world to "Woody," our food truck a few weeks later in October 2011.

With no restaurant experience, all the odds were against us. However, the mighty ONE was for us! It was a MASSIVE growth season as two "babies" were delivered one after another. A precious new baby boy and a startup food truck concept selling radical fish tacos. We fastened our seat belts!

In less than three months, Susan was working the front taking orders and filling in where necessary with our youngest swaddled closely to her. Scott was working 120+ hours a week. He was making zero dollars. Susan continued to cover where needed in between nursing a newborn and homeschooling the little ones. Wait, this wasn't the plan.

So-Cal Tacos was getting tons of exposure locally and nationally, and every chance given Scott was sharing his testimony. That was the plan!

Early 2012, Susan was introduced to an essential oil company and fell in love. She ordered oils and started this journey of learning how she could make an impact and empower other families with natural solutions. During this time she was frustrated with never being able to spend time with me and struggling to get the bills paid. Susan had a vision and was inspired to take the family finances in a different direction. She was even more determined and on a mission to change as many lives as possible, starting with her own family.

Soon, Susan found herself in front of thousands of people, all looking for the same thing. HOPE. HOPE for a family member, an illness, aches, pains, depression, the list goes on and on. Susan was now giving HOPE to others. That was the plan as well.

So here we were, a cancer survivor wearing a hat backwards, slinging tacos, and spreading love all around town and Susan educating folks about the power of essential oils. But wait, what about our sweet little angels? There were times when we'd kiss them goodbye early in the morning and not see them until they were already tucked in by the sitter. Our hearts wanted so badly to be the ones to tuck them in. When we didn't have a sitter, Susan would take all four little ones with her. She had to take a diaper bag, books, games, toys, and plenty of snacks. It was such a challenge and extremely difficult. This was definitely not part of the plan....Something needed to change.

Shortly after, we learned we would welcome the fifth Wooley to the world. With working overtime on both startups and making "next to no money," we were nervous about how we could make this all work? Remember when we said something had to change? Well, unfortunately, it did. The stress, countless hours of work, mental and physical fatigue all took its toll, and Susan miscarried only a few weeks after finding out we were pregnant.

Now, as we tried to pick up the pieces, Susan had several essential oil classes scheduled and no desire to teach them. She asked Scott to teach them. Scott replied, "How? When would I have the time? I didn't sign up for this! What would I teach people about oils?" Susan reminded him that she'd used essential oils on him for 15 years and told him just to share his personal experience and what the oils have done for our family.

So here Scott was, a real estate guy turned taco-ministry guy, in a room with a bunch of ladies, about to teach his first essential oil class. He was petrified! He turned around to face the crowd, and something supernatural happened. He saw himself, in 2010, in the eyes of the people in the room. Not only did he see their HOPE, but he saw the HOPE of the world in their eyes. There's that word again—HOPE! He had not seen the vision previously in Susan's essential oil business. He rushed home to share the experience with Susan. The minute he saw her, he gave her a huge hug and a sincere apology. "I understand now! This company is not just about building a business. It's about giving HOPE to the world, and there just happens to be an opportunity to create an incredible residual income, at the same time." Now with the Wooley's united on all fronts: tacos, professional network marketers, and homeschoolers, things began to happen—quickly.

Soon, we were informed our essential oil team was the largest in Texas. Next, we transitioned our taco concept to its first brick and mortar restaurant. Then came magazine covers and worldwide accolades. Television appearances and three national commercials. Today, we're a team in everything we do. Scott teaches a group of nine kids once a week in subjects ranging from Latin to the timeline since creation. Susan teaches a group of eight kids the same subjects. We manage our essential oil business together and So-Cal Tacos is in the process of taking things to the next level! We have a very hands-on approach to homeschooling our four little ones and have officially become mom and dadprenuers. As we reflect on what we thought was a storm, we can't help but see God's hand over every move we made. Either he was there with a gentle nudge, arms open, or welcoming us back to Him. He was always there!

When we think about the lessons learned during this time in our life, we can't help but to think of gratitude, focus, passion, intensity, perseverance, determination, grace and, most importantly, teamwork!

It would be extremely unfair for us to take credit for our success. The truth is, ALL the glory goes to God. He blessed us with everything! The concepts, the hard times, the lessons, the opportunities, and the victories. Additionally, he blessed us with AMAZING team members and partners. He always seemed to introduce the right person at the right time. It's our passion to use our experience, mistakes, and desire to guide as many folks as possible to a world of crushed goals and a laundry list of victories. All while designing a fulfilled life overflowing with dreams achieved.

The bottom line: the low hanging fruit is the ripest fruit on the tree, soon it will fall to the ground and expire. If you want fruit you can HARVEST and store for later, that fruit is at the top of the tree, and you must work for it. Often times, you must risk everything and go "out on a limb" to HARVEST it. If you really want to go BIG...you plant your own orchard! Hopefully, our story has given you seeds to plant in YOUR orchard! We shall harvest!

TWEETABLE
With the Wooleys united on all fronts: tacos, professional network marketers, and homeschoolers, things began to happen—quickly!

Scott and Susan Wooley are doling out hope via essential oils and serving up the freshest tacos in town. Their accomplishments redefine every day as their little "world-changers" become prepared to dominate lives they design. From broken homes and without education, this couple had the odds against them. But they believe when you have desire and when the mighty ONE is FOR you, ANYTHING is possible. Connect with the Wooleys on all social media channels.

www.yesitstheoils.com
www.eatsocaltacos.com
Instagram: scottwooleybringsit
Instagram: socaltacos
Twitter: socaltacos
Facebook: swooley

CHAPTER 10

The Re-Defined American Dream

by Ed and Bessie Goldin

Bess: Growing up as a first-generation American citizen in my Russian-speaking, Jewish household was anything but typical. My parents juggled being entrepreneurs and raising three children, all while working seven days a week and conducting most of their parenting by phone calls. Hard work was always instilled in my upbringing, and education was extremely important. Money was equated with happiness, and it was always a struggle because time doesn't wait. The path I was always given was to go to school, get good grades, go to college, find a great job, get a great paycheck, get married, have babies, and live happily ever after. In theory, it sounded pretty straightforward. Nobody prepared me for the horrible economy upon graduation from an accredited university, the dog-eat-dog corporate culture, the annual reviews and politics, the constant anxiety, the fear of being replaceable, health issues, and ultimately the heartache of leaving my newborn after six weeks to go back to work. There was nobody who could prepare me for questioning my purpose, my value to the universe, and my footprint.

Ed: I came to Maryland at the age of four from Riga, Latvia without a lick of English. Upon arrival in the United States, my parents divorced and my father remarried. I lived primarily with my dad, and he was adamant about doing well in school, going to college, getting an excellent job, buying a house with a white picket fence, paying taxes, working for 40 years, and dying—the ultimate American Dream.

My father was rarely home and worked long days. From a young age I started exploring different ways to make money and pitch in around the house. I did construction work, masonry, and eventually got a government job, which is the equivalent of hitting the lottery where I came from. Working for the government eventually became mundane, and the feeling of doing the same thing every day, over and over, was terrifying. I left that job to pursue a more entrepreneurial endeavor with mortgages but couldn't prepare myself for the markets crashing and starting over only a couple of years into my new business. The mortgage crisis rippled throughout every single household. Foreclosures spread like wildfire and the mortgage industry took a massive hit. I had to come up with something different to excel at and make a living after banks nearly ceased lending money to buyers.

Meeting my wife, Bess, and moving to New York changed so much for me. I got involved with recruitment for the advertising, technology, and media industry and eventually opened my own office. It gave me so much joy knowing that I could help somebody attain something they were hoping for and give them a means to their end. What I wasn't prepared for were the hours (I swore I would never work like my father did), the sadness in my wife's eyes the days when she returned to work from her maternity leave, and, ultimately, the struggle to succeed. Being a business owner is challenging. Often times, there would be months before I would receive payment. Slowly the bills began to pile up, and expenses started rising. The dream of a house with a white picket fence was moving further and further away.

Bess: A chance encounter transformed our lives forever. A stranger posted a picture on Facebook that intrigued me. At the time, I was severely struggling with my weight a year postpartum. My lowest point came after our daughter's first birthday when I cut myself out of every photo. I was feeling run down, sustained on 4-5 cups of coffee a day. I slept terribly and truly was coming home from my job without an ounce of energy to devote to my baby. I was severely stressed out and was seeing a physician for regular injections of cortisone into my scalp for stress induced alopecia, a condition where my hair was falling out in clumps. So many diets failed me in the past, and I felt like I lost control. I inquired about that stranger's post and from that point on, our lives have never been the same.

I've always found that I do better with support and involved Ed in my journey. I started dropping the weight I struggled with, started sleeping better, gained back the confidence I had lost for such a long time, had more energy that didn't rely on caffeinating myself constantly, and most importantly, I felt like a better mother when I was around my little girl. Ed also achieved significant success and truly fell in love with the products we were using. Several months in, Ed saw that random stranger who introduced me to my nutritional wellness program being congratulated for becoming a six-figure income earner in nine months. That intrigued him to further explore things.

Ed: Upon learning that there is an actual, exciting industry called network marketing, I was blown away at the concept of residual income and the entrepreneurial spirit. The concept of having your own virtual franchise where you are provided with tools, systems, and trainings was extraordinary. I was already in love with the products and the culture of the company, plus they had integrity, and the compensation was amazing.

What started off as getting a couple of hundred dollars into our bank account turned into something incredible. By being coachable and eager to learn, that couple of hundred dollars evolved to a couple of thousand dollars in time, and then continued significantly growing weekly. There was a week where I recall calling Bess at work and telling her I think the company made a mistake, there's an extra zero in our weekly paycheck, and I was going to deposit it before they realized there was an error.

The tide shifted completely when our second daughter came into this world. It didn't make much sense for Bess to work for somebody else, ask for permission to take our kids to the doctor, and rely on babysitters to hear our kids first words and see their first steps. We were in an incredibly comfortable position where she could to stay home with our kids and help with our newly-found "family business." Of course, we encountered our share of naysayers. What we did didn't fit into their idea of a path or success. We were there to prove them wrong.

Bess: It's been quite an adventure for us. I am so blessed in finding purpose in our life by serving others, helping people achieve their goals, having the time and freedom to live our lives by design, and never missing a moment. My heart explodes when I hear from a mother who thanks me for being able to tie her own shoelaces after years of asking her husband or kids for help. There are truly so many beautiful stories that get shared with me daily. The personal growth I have achieved since I was introduced to this industry is immense. Personal development, organization, and passion is imperative to success with what I do. I value my time, and the time I spend with my family is something that can never be taken away from me ever again. I utilized my strengths and abilities from my previous corporate America life in my everyday actions. There is a discipline to be had when being your own boss. While there is immense flexibility when it comes to working, the blinders go on and focus is key.

Ed: Growing a team of over 11,000 in four years has been awesome. Most importantly, being able to help other mothers and fathers find a way to supplement their income or reach some health goals is beyond rewarding. I love working alongside my wife and seeing that spark in her reignite. I enjoy checking off the boxes on the vision board we created. I don't take the time with my children for granted and whether we'll be able to play hooky from daycare and take our kids to a waterpark isn't something we need to worry about ever again. We've attained time, freedom, family, and fun through this incredible endeavor.

Bess and Ed: Our path may not have fit into the definition of the American dream, but we are beyond thrilled it didn't. While we chose a different path to success than we were taught as children, we feel we have found another way. A better way. A way that will leave our children a legacy from us, experiences that will be unforgettable, examples of perseverance and a lesson of service. Our marriage and our working relationship have been taken to a whole other level and we truly enjoy working on filling in the blanks with each other's strengths when one of us is weak. Collaborating has been so much fun! One thing is for sure, our house with a white picket fence is under contract our vision board is growing.

We learned to set negative emotions aside after hearing the "noise" around us from people who knew nothing about our family dynamic, financial situation, or passion. What we have now is worth the struggle we went through to overcome the resistance that met us along the way. The hard work, belief, and energy we put into our business has come full circle, and we are now living the American dream.

TWEETABLE
You are in charge of your own American Dream and the path to take you there.

Ed and Bessie Goldin are one of the fastest growing earners and top achievers with Isagenix. They found their vehicle to success by being at the service of others in achieving their goals. While helping their vision board come to life, they lead a team of thousands to create their own dreams. Their two daughters are their inspiration and driver.

edgoldin@hotmail.com
Bessie.goldin@gmail.com
Facebook.com/bessie.goldin
Facebook.com/ed.goldin
#lifestyelsofanetworkmarketer

CHAPTER 11

Giving Your Best in the Most Difficult Times

by Gbenga Asedeko

You can't give what you don't have. If you don't have peace you can't give peace, and if you don't have joy and happiness, you can't give joy and happiness. You can only give what you have. You are a gift to others. What is the quality of your gift? It's easy to give our best to others when things are going smoothly, but when we are going through the most difficult times, can we still give our best to the people in our lives?

I began my career in the early 90's at the age of 19 doing computer training at my uncle's computer company, Tentrix Nigeria Limited, one of the first computer companies in Nigeria. I trained CEO's, executives, and professionals how to use Microsoft Word, Excel, Access, and Desk Operating System (DOS). I found myself using life experiences to explain computer terminologies. Many of my students were inspired by my training.

There began my speaking career. Today, I speak to business, organizations, and schools with tremendous success. I am also a retirement planner, most of my work in the last year has been focusing on helping educators retire happy. My partner and I helped over 250 educators last year and we are on track to surpass that number this year.

Balancing business, family, and personal development have always been a manageable task for me. At the same time, when you add the challenges of life to an already busy schedule, things can easily become difficult and get out of control. January 17, 2015 was supposed to be a joyful day for my family and I. It was the day my wife gave birth to our son, Jaden G.Q. Asedeko, through C-section. Our son was in the hospital for several days because his oxygen level was very low. We were thankful for the bundle of joy and grateful that he would be fine after all the treatments given to him. My wife was in so much pain after the delivery of our baby. She told me that the pain was not normal, and that she felt like something else was going on. We shared the concern with the hospital, but we were told that the pain was normal due to the C-section. She was sent home on January 19, 2015. The pain got worse after we got home. We called the hospital. They said for her to continue to take the pain medication which was given to her.

On January 23, 2015, Jaden was released from the hospital. We were very happy to finally have the family together at home. Unfortunately, the following day I rushed my wife to the emergency room due to the pain and the eruption of a hematoma above the incision from the C-section. After the diagnoses, we were given the bad news by the doctor. My wife had been infected with three deadly, flesh-eating bacteria, and we were told that the bacteria might kill her due to how far they had spread. But, they would do their best to stop the bacteria from spreading all over her body. After two back-to-back, major surgeries, my wife was left with a big and deep open wound that covered half of her belly.

We were in the hospital for several days. While at the hospital, I called home to check on my seven-year-old son Jordan and our new baby Jaden. I heard everybody crying. Our dog, Panda, had been run over by a car and killed in front of Jordan. I rushed home and took our beloved dog for cremation. The psychological effects of what we were going through as a family in the space of two weeks kept piling on. Families, friends, and my church gave tremendous support during this difficult time, and we were very grateful.

We began the long recovery process and months of wound care. On July 1, 2015, the wound had closed and my wife was cleared to go back to work. We were very excited, but the excitement lasted for about a week. I got a call from Nigeria that my mom had died. The news took all the strength I had left in me. I was devastated, heartbroken, depressed, and restless, but I didn't give up hope. I was torn between traveling to Nigeria for my mom's funeral and staying with my wife and children who were still battling with the psychological effects of what we'd been through. After much deliberation, we decided the right thing to do was for me to go home to honor my beloved mom.

After the funeral, we continued as a family to piece our lives back together. After everything that happened, what is a catastrophe for most was just one more thing. On November 6, 2015, I was in a major car accident with an 18-wheeler. Thank God, I did not sustain any major injuries. At the same time, this caused us to lose the little momentum we'd gained in our recovery process.

All of 2016 was about getting back up and rebuilding every area of our lives. We had some setbacks with my wife's health, but we are standing strong. Every aspect of my life was affected during this challenging period. I was drained spiritually, financially, mentally, physically, and emotionally. My level of productivity went down drastically and I found myself not giving my best to my wife, to my children, to the people in my life, and to myself.

I quickly realized what had happened could not be an excuse to avoid giving my best in my relationships. Don't let life get the best of you, get the best out of life. When life gives you a lemon, don't only make lemonade out of it, make lemon cake, lemon lotion, lemon soap, and lemon chicken soup out of that lemon. Don't waste your pain, hurt, and disappointment, get the most out of them. You have it in you to win. You are made for more than enough. Whatever you are going through is no match for the greatness on the inside. Jim Rohn said, "You might not be able to change your life overnight, but you can change the direction of your life overnight." I made up my mind to change the direction of my life overnight, and I realized somebody somewhere is going through something worse than I.

I began by dividing my life into areas and focused on them one at a time. I developed a strong mental picture of success for every area of my life and began taking baby steps toward significant progress. One of the areas that was very important to me was the training, nurturing and teaching of my children, especially Jordan. He was greatly affected by what we went through. I developed a daily routine of praying with him and doing our daily success declaration together. Within few weeks, he brought his grades back up and finished the semester with honors.

What will truly help you to give your best in the most difficult times is one of the best lessons I learned during my difficult time. Don't make other people's problems your problems. I made the mistake of making what was going with my wife and my son, the loss of my mom, and the loss of my dog my problem. Thus, I was overwhelmed, frustrated, angry, unproductive, and giving the minimum, instead of my best, to the people in my life. Once I realized what was going on, I let go of their problems and began to focus on using the little energy left in me to rebuild my life. I stopped making my wife's illness my illness. I realized that I am not a doctor and I am not God. When I did, instead of having two sick people, one physically sick and the other emotionally sick, I become strong for my wife. I pray for them, support them, and make sure they get the right treatment. There is time for weeping together, but don't let their problem get the best of you. If you do, you have two sick people trying to help each other.

The principle of not making other people's problem your problem applies to different areas of our lives. If someone has a bad attitude, don't make their bad attitude become your problem. If you have a troubled child, don't allow his or her problem to become your problem. If you have a difficult employee, don't allow his or her problem to become your problem. If you are losing sleep over someone or something, you might be taking on other people's problems. When you make other people's problems your problems, it will prevent you from making good decisions. Taking on other people's problems will cause you to want to please them, and when you please others you can't give your best to them. Making other people's problem your problem will cause you to worry about what they think or say about you, and when you do, you can't give your best.

To give your best in the most difficult times, let go of other people and use the little energy you have left to build yourself up so you can give your best. You will have tremendous peace when you stop making other people's problems your problem. When you have peace, you have energy and focus. You will be productive and make good decisions. When you love others, you will not make their problems become yours, because you will be giving your best to them.

I truly believe that your tragedy can be turned into triumph, your dissatisfaction can be turned into your satisfaction, your disappointment can be turned into your divine appointment, your test and trials can become your testimonies, and your mess can be turned into a message which will influence millions and billions of people all over the world. I'm thinking about you. Remember, to never give up. You are a gift and you can give your best in the most difficult times. Choose to make every day a winning day!

TWEETABLE
Don't let life get the best of you, get the best out of life.

Gbenga Asedeko is a dynamic and enthusiastic motivational speaker, author, coach, and entrepreneur. Gbenga has served the city and county of El Paso, Sodexho Food Services, Spira Shoes, the real estate industry, colleges, universities, and school districts across Texas. For seminars, keynote speeches, coaching, and consistent, life-changing inspiration, contact Gbenga.

www.gbengaasedeko.com
gbenga@gbengaasedeko.com
Facebook: Gbenga R Asedeko
Twitter, LinkedIn, Instagram: Gbenga Asedeko

CHAPTER 12

It's Not About the Position: It's About the Mission

by Taylor Thompson

I was that girl from the other side of the tracks—you know, the one not likely to achieve much. I was the last person anyone expected to become who I am today: an international speaker, coach, and successful mompreneur. Even I did not imagine that I could be a trainer and coach who mentors women or that I could start up a company in my garage and grow it into a multimillion-dollar business.

One powerful and simple lesson I teach is that it's not about the position, it's about the mission. Sometimes the mission is hidden or takes time to grow. That's how it was with me.

I grew up in West Texas. My family lived in a mobile home and moved from trailer park to trailer park so often that I attended five different elementary schools. I always wanted more. I always had dreams. When I think about my dreams then, as a young girl, as a young woman, as a mother, as a single parent—those dreams were so much smaller than the reality of my life today, a life that is rich in what matters: marriage to my best friend, soulmate, and business partner, three smart and talented daughters to treasure, and professional success. And yet, without those small dreams of mine, in the beginning, I would still be that girl nobody expected could achieve success.

I was a latchkey kid. My mom was at work before I woke up in the morning, and I came home from school to an empty trailer until my parents returned from work. It wasn't an easy life, and I don't want any child ever to come home to an empty house.

I wouldn't change anything, though, for myself. My parents gave me love and strong values, even though we were blue collar and living in a trailer. It's because of the hardships I saw and lived through that I developed a strong desire to do and be something different.

I started by setting my sights on a college degree. There were no scholarships and no college savings account. Paying for college was on me, and I worked multiple part-time jobs to make it happen.

It was while I was in college that I met the man I thought was the man of my dreams. He was a star athlete and became a professional football player. Suddenly, I was the wife of a highly-paid and highly-respected National Football League player. Wow. Barely out of college and I had arrived. Right? I found my dream. Right? And when, after being married for a short time I found myself pregnant with our first daughter, it felt like the perfect life.

Then my husband had a career ending injury, and everything changed. We had a newborn baby and no income. We were forced to move from the exciting life we enjoyed in California back to West Texas and the kind of life I thought I had left behind forever.

Sometimes I'm sad when I think of those years, even though my greatest joy—my daughters—also happened then. We struggled as a couple, as a family. I bore three darling daughters even as our marriage gradually eroded and fell apart. My husband was controlling. His need to rule me slowly became emotional abuse. I think that his self-esteem never recovered from his failure as a pro football player, and he did not know how to channel his insecurities in a way that was not hurtful.

Momcare not Daycare

It's incredible to realize this, but even having lived through abuse and difficult years I feel blessed. I was able to use the negativity in my life as a springboard to something better. It was for my kids. I was determined and had a burning desire to provide my girls with momcare, not daycare.

Who knew that taking on the challenge of having a business at home would turn out to be one of my best decisions? And it started with a goal to make an extra $800 a month. That's all. $800. For my kids.

Why $800? That was simply the difference between momcare and daycare.

Figuring out how to earn money working from home was a big learning process, and there was no one to teach me. Twenty years ago, there were ads all the time. Work from home! Stuff envelopes! Make extra money! I did those. I answered almost every ad, including some that pertained to sales. Like everybody else, I was not interested in "selling" anything. I wanted to make extra money, but I did not like the thought of being a salesperson from home.

I tried all different types of work-from-home programs. I did crazy, crazy, things. I bought all sorts of programs. I made beaded earrings working from home. I actually processed angora goat hair out of my bath tub. I know that sounds crazy, but it's what they told me to do. They make doll hair with it. I was so naïve that I didn't realize most of the money-making and work-from-home programs are scams.

One ad really caught my attention, though. It told me a story about a couple who were making $10,000 a month working from home. What was interesting to me is that the couple lived close by where we were in West Texas. I remember thinking when I read that ad, Wow! Somebody in a small town, in a rural area like me, makes $10,000 a month? Surely, I can make enough to be a mom at home and keep my daughters out of daycare!

That's the mindset I had when I started my business: give my daughters momcare instead of daycare. I became a mompreneur. I went out and shared my story. I shared other people's stories. I shared the power of the product and its benefits, how it helped me. In my first month, I made three times my original $800 goal.

It is still amazing to me. I literally created a six-figure, international business around raising three little girls.

The sad part of life was still my marriage. My husband's negative attitude made it harder to grow my business, and it was a struggle to live in the tense, angry environment. But I learned a lot about business and personal growth. Emotionally and spiritually, I grew until I was in a different place than he was, and he didn't come along. My success only caused our problems to escalate.

I went from being a stay-at-home mom of three to being a single mom of three. It was not a decision made lightly. It was, however, the right decision for my girls and for me.

Mompreneur Success: If I Can Do it, You Can Do it!

Meeting and exceeding the needs of my children is my inspiration and motivation. As my business success grew, my personal growth bloomed exponentially. I love that I can do more for my kids and be a stronger model for them. Personal growth doesn't stop, you know. As I continue to grow, my girls grow. I have even more value now to share with my daughters because of the personal and business growth I've experienced.

Adversity is meant to be overcome. I have had many dark times in my life, some of which I've mentioned. In every case, it has been my business that provided (and continues to provide) the source of my emotional sustenance. By embracing the concepts I was being taught in my business along with being connected to all of the positive people surrounding me, I got through each dark day stronger for having been there.

My focus was on the daily method of operation (DMO), the process I follow to work my business. That focus is the support that led my business to a six-figure income in the midst of adversity. Even now, I follow this process and start my day early with quiet time with my Lord, exercise, and journaling.

Success, to me, is what money and time freedom allows me to do for my kids. I can't put a price on what it means that I am the person teaching them their values. From a truly humble start, just being focused on $800 a month, I have raised three beautiful daughters. One of them, my youngest one, just graduated this last year. It's been an absolute blessing having a business from home. It is my passion.

We have a lifestyle that allowed me to be with my children, to be present at all their activities, the cheerleading events, the volleyball games, the basketball games. How can I put a value on being involved in their schooling at every level? On knowing that I had a hands-on role in raising, in rearing? That I could instill my own value system in my children and not be forced to put learning integrity in the hands of somebody else? There is no monetary value that can be placed on the precious gift that being a successful mompreneur has given to my family and me.

When speaking to groups all over the world, my message is about balance. There are few things I love more than giving training and mentoring to like-minded business owners. I teach them by example, by being the best person I know to be, and by sharing the good and bad experiences in my life.

You know, I am so far away from a West Texas trailer now. When I speak and coach, it's about sharing how I overcame challenges. This story, my story, gives hope and guidance. My true success has been to raise my daughters and continue helping so many others achieve their dreams and goals. Truly, if I can do it, then anyone can do it.

I am unashamed and passionate about sharing my story. It comes from deep within my soul and from a place of gratitude. I love sharing with other moms who want to be home with their children. I love sharing with anyone who has the drive and desire that I feel.

I have stepped far outside of my comfort zone. That's what it takes. Achievement takes doing the things that are uncomfortable even more than doing what comes naturally. You can do it, too. You can have the same kind of success I've had.

How? It comes down to having a burning desire to make a difference. Be willing to do the work necessary. Do it yourself or get help, just get it done. Focus on your daily method of operation (DMO). Be teachable and willing to look in the mirror and ask, "How can I be better? What can I do differently tomorrow to make myself better? What can I do to make a difference in someone else's life? To grow my business?" Focus on the process, the daily steps that keep you moving forward; when you focus on your family and you focus on how you can bring value to lives of others, you can have a strong business and be successful no matter what.

Who I am today comes from accepting nothing less than momcare instead of daycare. If not for my kids, I would have never chosen to start a business in my garage. And that's led me to my mission: to share my story and continue to be a walking example of what's possible, for my girls and the people I work with.

TWEETABLE

"It's Not About the Position; It's About the Mission"
International Speaker/Coach Taylor Thompson
#mompreneur #momcarenotdaycare

Taylor Thompson began her career out of necessity and a simple desire to stay at home to raise her children. She built a six-figure business while raising three daughters and discovered her niche. Working with and coaching single parents and stay-at-home moms is also her passion. Her experience and instincts have translated into successful training strategies. Taylor now works internationally and in partnership with husband Larry and can be found online at https://www.facebook.com/larryandtaylor/.

CHAPTER 13

A Life of Simple Choices

by Todd Falcone

"Life is better when you can afford to make the choices YOU want WHEN you want them." That's been my motto for as long as I can remember.

They say that "money can't buy happiness"…and it's true. I have plenty of friends who have all the money in the world, but no happiness. What money DOES buy is the freedom to make choices on how you live your life. The happiness is up to you…because more money certainly doesn't "buy" it.

Before I was ever even thinking of being a parent, I wanted to have the freedom to choose how I lived my life. I didn't know exactly HOW that was going to happen, but I did know that I wanted a life that provided choices.

I grew up in a very middle-class household that had no entrepreneurs in my family. None of my upbringing was moving me toward being a self-employed man.

However, I was very fortunate to be introduced to network marketing at a very young age. When I was 22 and getting ready to graduate from college, I got introduced to the business model, and it was something I had never even heard of before. So, I went in with an open mind and a clean slate. No opinions, no misconceptions, and no one giving me their opinion about it.

It made sense to me…so I did it.

Fast-forward 26 years later…I'm still here. I've invested my entire business career being an at-home entrepreneur in network marketing and now spend all of my business time speaking and training on the things that worked well for me in the field as an active distributor.

When I was asked to contribute a chapter for this book, I wanted to make sure that the message I conveyed was something that people could easily grasp, and come to the understanding that it CAN happen for you as well, if you're willing to do a few simple things. I said simple…not easy. Remember that.

Here's what I want to share with you about being a husband, a father, and an entrepreneur who has all the time in the world to spend with the ones he loves most.

Life is too short not to enjoy every moment you can with the people you love the most.

We spend such a big part of our lives working. In fact…most people spend far more time working than they do with their kids or their spouse. You have to make the conscious decision to free up time to do the things that matter the most, even if you do it in an employed environment. If you don't, you most certainly will end up doing what most people do…and that's working all the time and waking up one day realizing your kids are grown and gone.

About 8:30 in the morning one day, I was in my front yard playing basketball with my oldest boy. There were all sorts of cars leaving their driveways and exiting the neighborhood. My kid says to me, "Dad, where's everyone going this morning?"

I had to laugh because he didn't know. His dad has always worked from home. I said, "Buddy, they're all going to work!" He says to me, "You mean they don't all work from home like you do?"

I replied, "No Gianni…they have a job they go to every day."

My son said, "Dad, I like your job better!"

That conversation is something I'll never forget, and it's the kind of experience you can have when you choose a vehicle that enables you to work from home and create your own schedule.

Our family loves camping, and apparently, a LOT of other families do too! However, we don't like getting stuck in traffic on a busy camping weekend. One of the greatest things about being self-employed and on your own schedule is the simple choice of leaving when you want, not when the boss says you can.

This may seem like a trivial benefit, but when we do a weekend camping trip with the family, we leave on a Wednesday or Thursday (avoiding Friday camp traffic), and stay at our campsite until Monday or Tuesday. It's quiet.

Let me share with you a few things that I think you'll find useful on your journey to creating the life you want so you can do whatever it is you like to do with your loved ones.

Seven Simple Ideas to Create Success in your Life

#1: Find Something You Can Get Excited About.
Whatever you choose to pursue, it's got to be something that fires you up and makes you want to do it. If you dread your occupation, you're not going to go as far as someone who LOVES what they do.

#2: Think Long-Term.
Too often, I see people get into business for themselves and treat it as a "short-term, part-time plaything." You have to be whatever you are in for the long-haul. Success takes time, and you have to exercise patience along the journey. I didn't make money for my first two years! If I had a short-term view, I wouldn't even be writing this!

#3: Follow the Success of Others.
There are plenty of people to model, to follow, and to emulate. Find someone you have respect for that has had success in whatever you are pursuing and do your best to replicate what they've done. There's never a need to re-invent the wheel. One of the greatest lessons I've ever learned is this: when someone has something that you want, and they're willing to show you exactly how they did it…DO it, and don't change a thing! People always want to put their own spin on something they've never done before. Create some success doing it the way someone else has already proven it can be done, then add your own personality to if it if you want.

#4: Dinner, Soccer, and Hugs Take Priority.
I'll stop work for a hug or a kiss from my wife or kids at any moment. Sitting down to dinner and connecting with my family is something that is important to me. Yes…I miss dinners because of meetings or conference calls, but I also plan my personal life around my business schedule to afford the time to spend with them. No matter what you do, there's always time for hugs, soccer games (or whatever your kids do), and family meals.

#5: WORK is a Good Four-Letter Word.
Success takes work…period. Your ability to hustle, roll up your sleeves, and get after it, is what's going to get you there. When I work, I work HARD. When I play, I play hard. Laziness never pays the bills. Even if you don't have a lot of talent, you can outwork other people around you and still get ahead in life. You'll get better along the journey if you work on getting better. But still, there's nothing better than good, old-fashioned sweat equity to get ahead in life.

One more thing. The vehicle you choose matters. Most people work hard, but, finding a vehicle (like network marketing) provides you leverage that lots of other careers don't. If you're going to work hard in life, you might as well work hard in something that has a big payoff rather than something that doesn't.

#6: Sharpen Your Saw Daily.

Whatever you are doing requires you being the best you can possibly be at it. A big mistake a lot of people make is not specifically dedicating time to improving their craft. If you wanted to play professional golf, you'd practice. If you want to be a professional entrepreneur, you need to practice. It's that simple. Look at your schedule. Are you setting dedicated time aside to work on getting better? Or, are you simply doing? Most people do but don't work on what they're doing. That's not a good recipe for long-term success.

#7: Reward Yourself.

I've said it before. I work HARD. There are some days I'll put 16 hours in… straight. Not every day is spent playing with my kids. That's called being in business and having the responsibilities that go along with it. However, I always build rewards in for myself. If I've had a big few days of work, I'll set aside an entire day to play with my boys, watch movies, or take them someplace fun.

By the way, this goes for spouses as well. My wife and I have a date night almost every week. And when I say almost…we rarely miss one. I've seen relationships go by the wayside over business far too many times. I've been with my wife now for over 24 years, and that relationship takes work and deserves attention.

Losing a spouse or having a marriage that falls apart over work can be easily avoided if you simply tend to that garden. Every garden needs watering. Take the time if you're married and reading this to nurture that relationship. My marriage hasn't always been easy, but I can tell you that we're in a better place today than we ever have been. And, it's because we've worked on it.

Some Final Thoughts…

Take my advice on this one. Years ago when I was working for my family's radio station, I knew an old man named Jack. He'd pull up and work the night shift at the station. At the time, Jack was probably 80 years old and drove a car that barely ran.

He said to me, *"Todd…don't be like me. Save your money. I'm too old to be working, but I still have to work. You don't want to be like me. Save your money kid."*

I took what Jack said to heart and began putting money aside, even when "I thought" I couldn't afford to do so.

No matter how good your business is going, it always rains. That phrase we've all heard in our lives, "save for a rainy day," is one you should remember. It rains everywhere. Be ready for it. You'll thank me later if you heed this advice and pay yourself first.

Lastly, I'll say this. You WILL BE challenged. You'll want to "throw in the towel," surrender or quit during your time as an entrepreneur.

Don't do it. Don't give up. The only time you'll truly fail is when you give up. Every successful person I have ever met has been faced with roadblocks, challenges, and failures, but it's the moments you push through them that make the biggest difference for your business.

Family and friends are so important to me, and spending time with them is what matters the most. You deserve to have the best life you want...for you.

It takes work, long-term commitment, humility, and a never ending hunger to make whatever you are doing work. Stay with it, and you'll look back one day and know that it was all worth it!

TWEETABLE
You WILL BE challenged. You'll want to "throw in the towel," surrender, or quit during your time as an entrepreneur. Don't do it. Don't give up.

Todd Falcone has over 25 years of experience in the network marketing profession. With it, he carries a strong passion for the industry and what it has to offer. Over the past decade, he's dedicated all of his time to teaching people how to succeed in network marketing. His distinctive style of candid, in-your-face presenting layered with comedy and practical instruction has his audiences both laughing and learning at the same time. To learn more, visit http://www.ToddFalcone.com

CHAPTER 14

Paratroopers Turned Full-Time Family

by Daniel and Tara Parten

To say my husband and I took an unconventional path to where we are today is a major understatement. Daniel and I met while we were both cadets at the United States Military Academy at West Point, a place where our young love had to take a backseat to the rigorous academic, physical, and military demands. After we graduated and were commissioned as Officers in the US Army, we found a small window of time to get married in between our demanding military duties such as Ranger School for Daniel, Airborne School for us both (though at different times), and many other requirements that consistently consumed our time, our focus, and our spirits.

Our lives were very unlike most college graduates, and we were never able to experience our "newlywed" or "honeymoon" phases, as they were overtaken by demanding Army training and countless months apart, usually with no or very little ability to communicate. The most challenging event was when we both went on a combat deployment to Afghanistan, where we were each individually responsible for the lives and well-being of our platoons, roughly 25-50 soldiers each.

To add to my stress, Daniel's platoon was one of the most combat-facing platoons in the region. And what was worse, on a daily basis, I had access to the casualty reports. Although my logical brain didn't want to read them, my heart had to, and so every day as I scrolled through the reports, I would be numb until I was positive Daniel was not among the list of names. Thankfully Daniel remained safe, though he did lose soldiers in his unit, and in our last month overseas, we lost one of our West Point classmates, who was our best friend. Unfortunately, this type of loss was not new to us. Three years prior, in 2009, Daniel's older brother and best friend, Tyler, was killed in combat during his own deployment.

All these events were overwhelming. They happened during our developmental years, before either of us were 25 years old, and on top of that, we were still "newlyweds!" I had gone from a girlfriend who was trying to help my grieving boyfriend cope, to a wife who didn't know what her role was anymore. On the other side of our relationship, Daniel was broken. In his words, "My brother and I were so close that when he was taken from this earth, my spirit went with him." He was psychologically and emotionally on autopilot, in pure survival mode, just going through the motions.

Although we each had consciously and voluntarily chosen our career and were incredibly grateful to serve our great nation, the ebb and flow of catastrophic events that transpired in such a short amount of time left us and our relationship hanging by a thread. We had spent less than 50% of our marriage together and we were both unfulfilled, without drive, and passionless. It was almost as if, at this point, we were simply coexisting, without much left in our tanks to offer each other. We were headed down two completely separate paths that were going to take us further and further away from each other, not just geographically, but also emotionally. It was all certain to pull us apart.

We knew we needed change and we needed it soon, but we honestly had no clue what that would look like, and we weren't even sure where to start. But God works in wonderful ways. That was the time entrepreneurship came into our lives in the form of network marketing. As millennials, we were completely unaware that this industry even existed, and therefore we had no idea just how much it could bless our lives. But, we knew enough to be intrigued, and so we dug deeper.

It was then that Daniel attended a major educational/training event so we could do our own due diligence by seeing the opportunity, the culture, and the company leadership with our own eyes and make an educated judgment call on whether or not it was right for us. Today, I am so glad he did because I will never forget what happened when he walked in the door after he returned home. He sat me down on our couch, held my hands, looked into my eyes, and told me, "Baby, I don't need to keep pursuing my Special Forces career anymore. This is what we've been praying for, a way for us to build our lives together. I know we can do this." As tears streamed down my face, I knew God had answered my prayers, because I had not seen that much hope and belief in Daniel's eyes since we had first met, before we endured so much hardship. I knew this was going to require a lot of hard work and perseverance, and it would require us to "go against the current" of the conventional career path. But I had a gut feeling it would be worth it and our family would prosper like never before, which is exactly what we desperately needed.

We weren't wrong. This profession and industry, through hard work and determination, brought so much life back into our household. In a very short amount of time we were able to pay off our debt in full without having to dip into our personal savings, which felt incredible and gave us so much more financial breathing room! We were now aligned with a company and immersed in a culture of strong belief where it was not just accepted, but encouraged, to cast a bold vision for what we wanted for our future and to pursue it with our whole being. With that level of belief and positive mindset, our marriage began to thrive because we had so much more of ourselves available to give to each other. Now that our individual hearts were full, we were there for each other in ways we could not be before. What we were pursuing aligned seamlessly with our values of high integrity, made health a priority, and had a family-first atmosphere where we felt supported in what we believed and who we were at our core.

Most of all, what we truly wanted was to be together and to grow our wealth and our future together. We no longer wanted to see each other only on the weekends, or at the end of the day when work had gotten the best of us and we could only give what was left of us to each other. And on top of that, we truly wanted to grow our family, but we didn't want someone else raising them while we were both at work 60+ hours a week. We knew there had to be another way, a better way! We were so grateful for the opportunity to have served our country, but for our family, it was time for a new chapter, and our hard work in our personal business afforded us that ability. That was when we both left the military.

Daniel went to work for a global consulting firm, but thankfully, because of the hard work we had done with our network marketing business, I was able to transition to being a full-time entrepreneur. And with our tiny addition to our family (our little girl!), I am now officially a full-time mompreneur!

In this new and fulfilling role, I have been able to be home and fully present with our daughter Denver, all while contributing to our household income. This opportunity has given me the ability to leverage my time to build an income that will soon bring Daniel home with us too, fulfilling our vision of being a "full-time family." I get to choose the hours I work my business and the hours I spend away from my baby. It's not always easy, but having the power to make our own decisions instead of having our decisions made for us has been the biggest gift to our family!

In hindsight, we are so grateful for our hardships because we are now in a place where we have so much to offer other families. We know that if we were in the desperate situation we were in, there are thousands of others in this world feeling the same way—lost, not in control, and unfulfilled. Because of that conviction, we are now on a mission to show other people that they have the power to create options and flexibility for themselves and their families. Not only do they have the ability, they deserve it! We are advocates for intentional living, and we empower families to realize they have control and a responsibility to choose what they want their future to look like.

We will be the first to say that anything worth having must be earned, so it certainly will require hard work. But as Daniel and I know all too well, life is short—too short, in fact, to spend it feeling stuck or doing anything other than what makes you come alive. The reality is, we can spend our lives building our dreams or someone else's, but we have the power to choose which one. It's time to take ownership of our decisions and start moving towards a life of intention, a life on purpose. We did it, and so can you.

TWEETABLE

Life is short—too short to spend it feeling stuck or doing anything other than what makes you come alive. #veterans #family #purpose

Daniel and Tara Parten are West Point graduates, former Army Officers and Combat Veterans, who experienced significant adversity. They realized life is too short to spend it doing anything other than what makes you come alive, so they changed their trajectory. They are now entrepreneurs, network marketers, and proud parents of a beautiful baby girl. They are advocates for intentional living and are on a mission to show others that they have the power to create a life of choice for themselves.

www.danielandtaraparten.com
Instagram: taraparten
          danielparten
Facebook.com/partentara
Facebook.com/partendaniel
Email: partentara@gmail.com
          partendaniel@gmail.com

CHAPTER 15

Freaky Friday

by Joanne Moretti

My story is about a role reversal, but I didn't switch places with my daughter, although that would be interesting. My story also starts in a Chinese restaurant on a Friday, while we were trying to have dinner and, at the same time, figure out what we were going to do about the fact that my husband, Anthony's, sales kick-off in Las Vegas was at the same time as my senior leader meeting in NYC.

This predicament was getting all too "normal" now that both of us had completed our parental leave and were back at work full time. When we were both out of town at the same time, our stress levels and anxiety would go off the charts. And, as a result, we would get caught up in non-productive bickering.

That particular Friday, as we frantically chowed down on the rice noodles with beef and black bean sauce, we both had an epiphany: *Why are we doing this? I mean really, why are we stressing out so much, and why would we leave our precious children in the hands of some vaguely familiar acquaintances when we really didn't have to?*

I could see my question reflected in his eyes. That's how in tune we've always been with one another. That's the freaky part. We not only had the same question running through our minds at the same time, we came to the same conclusion at the same time.

And that was really the moment, the earth shook, the bell clanged, the wind blew, and our spirits fully united as one team, one unit, one brain. We looked at each other and both said, "We don't." "Freaky Friday," as we call it in my home, was the day we said, "Enough. It's time for one of us to stay home."

Therein began the negotiation and deliberation. And the decision making. And the decision was clear: after a very long and successful career at Microsoft, Anthony said, "I'm good, you keep going. You're on a roll, and you love what you do." I was so happy with this choice and his bravery, I nearly jumped out of my chair and spilled sweet and sour sauce all over me!

That was the choice I was hoping he/we would make, and to this day, 14 years later, we both agree it was the greatest decision we've ever made. We brought these innocent kids into this world, and they deserved a parent at home with them not two parents traveling constantly with no fixed address.

Our logic was simple, "If we are at a point where we can afford for one of us to stay home, why on earth wouldn't we do it?" And frankly, the stress it relieved for me, knowing he was at home doing homework with the kids, making them meals every night, taking them to lessons, and generally watching them like a hawk, unlocked my full potential as a professional and allowed me to double my income within two and a half years.

So, the big lesson is, two parents working hard and on the go can be dilutive to their marriage, their parenting, and their careers. For us, one parent working full tilt and the other parenting full tilt allowed us to maximize one income to beyond what the two of us combined were making!

The other incredible benefits we saw were things like improved manners, grades, eating habits/health, and emotional disposition in our kids. Not to sound overly proud, but my kids are pretty awesome thanks to my husband's incredible parenting during the week and me taking over on the weekends.

In fact, we created a weekend ritual, pajama day one day, where I played and watched TV with the kids all day in our PJs, and the other day we went on an excursion.

Our weekends were definitely not freaky, and the memories we created are still vivid in our minds to this day.

The final lesson I will share is this, stay aligned. The thing that helped us through this journey was our sense of teamwork and unified approach to everything. If kids see a "crack of light through the wall" they will slide through it. In other words, be a wall, be solid and so tightly aligned, there are no cracks of light or "outs." In this world of uncertainty, the kids not only want to see their parents aligned, they need them aligned and parenting 24/7!

TWEETABLE

Freaky Friday: check out my chapter in #momanddadpreneurs on #parenting roles being reversed & the #family & #financial impact to our lives!

Joanne Moretti has 30+ years in the high-tech industry and is proud to be on the executive leadership team at Jabil, a 180k person/18b dollar design, manufacturing, and supply chain services company. Joanne serves as chief marketing officer, a corporate executive, and the general manager for Jabil's design firm, Radius. Joanne is a recognized advocate for the development and growth of women in STEM-related industries and business. Joanne, her husband, and their two children reside in Dallas, TX. All born and raised in Toronto.

joanne.moretti@gmail.com
Twitter: @JoannMoretti
Facebook: /joanne.moretti.12
LinkedIn: Joanne Moretti

CHAPTER 16

Brave and Passionate
A Better Life for My Girls

by Angela Maresca

I grew up in an immigrant household in Brooklyn, New York to two young parents from Lvov, Ukraine. They came to America in 1974 for a better life and greater opportunities than were available to them. When my mom first came to this country, she worked in a doll factory for $2.00 an hour. My stepfather was a taxicab driver, and both hardly knew any English, but their tireless work ethic and passion drove them to create a better life for us. Throughout my life, my parents emphasized that hard work and getting a good education was the #1 priority in life, and that, without it, you could not have a bright future. My parents believed that if you worked hard and got a great education you would be successful, but that was not the case. I worked to pay bills and lived from paycheck to paycheck. I couldn't seem to get ahead no matter how hard I tried.

My parents were ecstatic that I had found a job with a pension and benefits when I got a job with the NYC Administration for Children's Services investigating child abuse and neglect. I was thrilled to have joined a profession where I got to help people every day. I continued to work on my master's degree, then proceeded to work on my Ph.D. so that I could live up to my parents' dreams and earn a supervisory position.

I worked as a caseworker for five years. It was one of the most difficult jobs in the world. I knew I wanted to help people, but this was dangerous, low-paying, and thankless. There just had to be more out there. However, when I became a mother, investigating child abuse became difficult emotionally. I could not bear the thought of leaving my child with strangers after witnessing some of the things that went on in the field, nor could I put my infant in daycare. It was not right for my family financially or emotionally. Unfortunately, in today's workforce, many parents are faced with the choice of either working full-time or being a full-time parent.

After spending many years in school and carrying more than $70,000 in student loans, I left my job and became a stay-at-home mom, dependent on my husband's truck driver's salary. I was worried when I left this city job. I was losing the pension, the benefits, my independence and, most importantly, an opportunity to help people. I did not know if we would be able to survive on one income or what I would do the rest of my life. It was scary, especially with a new baby. I loved being a mom and still do, but every so often I would get the feeling that maybe, just maybe, I was meant for something more. I stayed home with my children without any income. Being unfulfilled and, quite frankly, a little bored, I started gaining weight. The pounds came on little by little, but my weight gain accelerated after I had my second child. By age 38, I had tried every weight loss program and fad diet on the market. I was exhausted and frustrated.

By the grace of God, I saw someone discussing their weight loss on social media and I decided to give their program a try. I expected to fail with this program as I have dozens of times. My husband even said to save the receipt so I could return it and get my money back. I was desperate for a change, and I prayed to God that this would work. Surprisingly, the program was easy, and the weight was falling off. Quickly, I experienced my own results like weight loss and energy gain, so I began sharing with family and friends. The more I shared, the more joy I felt.

My friends and family and those close to me saw my passion and excitement and decided to give the program a chance. Funny, but my husband, the skeptical one, dropped 11 pounds and quickly became a believer. This was so exciting to see the people in my life getting healthy together.

When a credit card came to my mailbox with $212 of earnings, it was the cherry on the cake! I was pretty excited that, as a stay-at-home mom, I was able to bring in some money for my family while helping others. My business totally rekindled my passion for helping people, which I had put on hold when I had given up being a caseworker. I had become the greatest cheerleader and coach to my friends and family on their journey of health, weight loss, and financial freedom.

I'd never heard of network marketing, but it didn't take long to see the benefits of getting my products paid for, and even earning a few extra hundred dollars. It did not take long before I hit a six-figure income and started enjoying the freedom that came with it. I was finally able to pay for camp for my children without a payment plan and even bring my entire family on a vacation paid for by me. Little by little the stress began to fade and the time freedom and happiness began to grow.

Discovering a way to help people, stay at home with my kids, and earn an income at the same time was like finding solid gold. I want to offer a life to my daughters where they can grow up and be whoever they choose to be in this world as long as they help other people. I want my daughters to know anything they dream is possible. I want to make my parents proud that the chance they took on moving to a new country and that their belief, hard work, and passion did not go in vain. I want to help many more people on my team make a multiple-six-figure income, so that they too can live the lives of their dreams. I want people to talk freely about the profession of network marketing and be proud of who they are. I don't know any other industry where you can become a top income earner in a short time with no financial cap. Long before I believed in myself, the beautiful profession of network marketing poured education, knowledge, and belief into me. Because I was brave, passionate, and wanted a better life for my girls, I refused to give up, and in four years, I became the 193rd company millionaire, became the top enroller, have personally helped over 600 people, bought our first home out of the city, and retired my amazing husband. If a stay-at-home mom from Brooklyn can do this, anyone can do this. Believe in yourself.

TWEETABLE
If a stay-at-home mom from Brooklyn can become a millionaire and retire her husband before 45, anyone can. Believe in yourself.

Angela Maresca became Isagenix's 193rd company millionaire at 41. Formerly a caseworker with New York City, Angela has become the #1 recruiter with Isagenix, retired her husband, and bought their first home through network marketing. Angela has won numerous trips to Paris, Rome, and Maui, but she is most proud of is the time freedom she gets to experience with her family.

917-501-3398
Qtang22@aol.com
https://www.facebook.com/qtang2211

CHAPTER 17

The Opportunity to Leave a Legacy

by Ron Miller

When my dad was 19 years of age, his dad died from drinking too much alcohol while being a diabetic. And, at that time, my dad's mom was in a mental hospital being treated for schizophrenia and was not fit to raise children. My dad was left along with his two younger siblings in Kansas City, Kansas to figure out how they were to make a living and find a place to live on their own. My dad's dad was a great salesman, and my dad inherently is also a great salesman. My dad used his sales skills and work ethic and worked three jobs as a painter, ski instructor, and dishwasher to make ends meet for him and his family. It's through action and trial and error that he became a success. He is never afraid to take the first step.

My story is starkly different. I was born and raised in Jackson Hole, Wyoming, one of the most beautiful places on earth. My parents are healthy and supportive and have been my entire life. They gave me and my three siblings every opportunity to succeed. My parents create a legacy by teaching and leading me and my siblings to think differently. Leaving a legacy means passing on a paradigm, thoughts, and values to future generations. For example, conventional wisdom is to go to school, get a job, work really hard, and invest for the long term in a 401(k), IRA, or mutual fund and hope and pray that at some time around 65 years of age you are able to retire. I do not see the business and investing world through this lens largely due to my dad's influence.

In 1997, my dad read the small purple book *Rich Dad Poor Dad* by Robert Kiyosaki and shortly after began operating several successful businesses and investing in real estate. Ever since, he has been an entrepreneur, never to return to a day job again. My dad leads by example for his kids. My dad does not force the paradigm, thoughts, and values shared in *Rich Dad Poor Dad* on us. He simply lives them. Being an entrepreneur can come with many perks including the freedom to spend your time on things that you want to. I remember countless fishing trips, camping adventures, and time spent at home together with my parents when I was a young boy.

These memories are priceless, and time spent together with family plays an important role in the vibrancy of our family today.

My dad gifted me *Rich Dad Poor Dad* to read at the age of 18. This gift marks a turning point in my life when I began a lifetime inquiry into personal development. My inquiry into personal development attracts countless mentors into my life. My mentors guide me by providing principles in life and business that work. I will share a few of these principles with you that have had a large impact in my life and hopefully they will do the same in yours.

Change your habits, change your life. I learned that using self discipline to form good habits creates huge positive momentum in anything in life that I choose to be, do, and have. One example is the habit I have of reading at least one hour every day. Carrying out this habit, I read about 50 books in a year. The books are full of new knowledge and change my life in a positive way.

Increased Education = Decreased Risk. To take this thought one step further and to borrow a term from The Real Estate Guys, I use education for effective action. We live in a time where there is no excuse for incompetence since we all have access to countless sources of education on the internet, so I take advantage of that. And then I do something! I lean into fear, take action, and learn lessons.

Learn from other people's mistakes and understand that I do not have to give natural childbirth to ideas; I can adopt other people's ideas. A mentor of mine once told me that she was so busy making things happen in her business that her kids grew up, and she regretted not spending more time with them. I adopted that lesson from my mentor and will not be making the same mistake. This same mentor taught me to never be afraid to ask for help. She taught me that I don't know what I don't know. People are very eager to help me when I ask.

Be, do, have. If I want to have something in life, the place I start is to ask: who do I need to *be* in order to *do* what it takes to *have* what I want? I am love in order to love my family and to have a loving household environment. My successes as a father, entrepreneur, and investor are a reflection of who I am.

My and my dad's contrasting stories are a testament that anyone can become a success no matter what their circumstance. I am, however, ever grateful that my mom and dad choose to design their lives in a way that creates an environment of success not only for themselves but for their family too. I may not have found any of my mentors or their guiding principles had it not been for my parents creating that environment of success.

The love of my life Kristy and I came home with our first child, a baby boy, whom we named Hugh Benjamin Miller. My first thought: what an opportunity to pass on a paradigm, thoughts, and values! Kristy and I have more influence on our boy than anyone else, especially now during the early stages of his life. As a father, I train, teach, and lead by example. I live with intentional habits and with a paradigm that love and freedom are expressions of who I am. I spend quality time with my family and play an active role in raising my son. Being an entrepreneur and investor allows me the freedom to work at home and spend more time with my family. I do not miss out on the moments that only happen once in a lifetime. I never stop learning and understand now more than ever that the teacher often learns more than the student. I am so grateful for the opportunity to leave a legacy.

TWEETABLE

"Who do I need to be in order to do what It takes to have what I want?"

Ron Miller has served as the Chief Operating Officer and Head of Business Development at Jackson Hole Reservations, LLC (jacksonhole.net) and Jackson Hole Real Estate Company, LLC (jacksonholerr.com) helping visitors, new residents, and investors in the beautiful Jackson Hole area. Ron's passion lies in business and real estate investing and he focuses on making positive impacts within his community of family, friends, neighbors, and fellow investors. Contact Ron on Facebook at facebook.com/ronalddavidmiller or call +1 (307) 200-8766.

CHAPTER 18

Broken Mom and Broken Back to Super Mom and Super Fit

by Sarah Rhew

Has life ever been so overwhelming for you that you wished you could bury your head in the deepest, darkest hole in the ground, praying that when you reappear, EVERYTHING would be gone? Do you find yourself preparing for the battlefield you call life every single day? I can relate. I am going to share experiences that have required me to make difficult decisions and that changed my direction altogether.

The ongoing joke amongst my friends is that I am a person who exudes light, love, and joy wherever I go. Most days, I choose to show up as myself, but the reality is that it is a moment-to-moment CHOICE. This world for me to exist in is more pleasant than one associated with pain and reality. I chose this world, and it has become my "armor" that I have taught myself to wear every day.

I was that typical high school student trying to figure out my place in the world. I felt so alone. Can you relate? I couldn't talk to my parents; I didn't feel like they understood me. I didn't have friends. I remember feeling awkward, unwelcome, and lost. This phase launched everything for me. I hurt so bad that my heart literally felt pain. I wanted out. I went to the medicine cabinet, removed a bottle of Tylenol, walked across the field to a classmate's house, and ingested the entire bottle. I recall my classmate talking about her latest drama. I politely nodded, smiled, and supported her on the outside. On the inside, I was experiencing a tornado of thoughts and emotions. Did I make a mistake? Will this be painful? Will anyone miss me? I remember going home, saying "goodnight" to my parents, and slipping away to my room. I recall thinking, "Will they figure it out?"

I didn't recognize the girl in the mirror. The one who looked back at me was pale, weak, and defeated. I tucked myself into bed and slipped away into a deep sleep. When I woke up, the first thought in my head was "SHIT! Why am I still here? What do I do now?" I had not prepared for this outcome. Life throws curve balls, and although we think we know the best path for ourselves, there is something greater at play.

What did I learn? Contrast is necessary in our lives: good, bad, highs, and lows. We cannot have one without the other. This was my first glimpse into the importance of communication. I felt empowered to become a more effective communicator and to cope with contrast. I gained vision and was enabled to take my future into my own hands.

How selfish of me to try to take my own life. If I had been successful, I would not have a child who makes me proud every single day. I would not have impacted the thousands of lives that I have. Most importantly, I wouldn't be here on this planet to serve in the capacity I am serving and witness the immeasurable impact of that.

If you feel lost, unaccepted, awkward, or are contemplating life, you are not alone. You are so loved, you are significant, you are on this planet for something bigger than you, and this is simply a season. Get the support you need, find the learning lessons in your situation, and keep moving forward. This is preparation for the next season.

I was young, early 20's, and I was standing right outside of the entry doors of a local grocery store. It was midafternoon on a crisp fall day; I was gripping my toddler's hand. I remember a feeling of complete mortification. There were families passing by me in the parking lot. I remember their faces, and I remember feeling so small. That moment made me want to disappear. I was being berated. I don't remember the reason. Usually it was for something as simple as not doing a task perfectly the way he expected or accusations of looking in the direction of another man. The reason doesn't matter. I just wanted to disappear. This is the time I decided to protect myself emotionally. I consciously remember building walls around my emotions to protect myself from pain and to begin numbing the damage.

I find it fascinating how women often feel it necessary to stay in situations that don't serve them, but when it begins to affect their children, they make a change. It happened with me. I continued to build walls day after day. I felt strong. I decided I was a survivor. But, let's be honest. All I was, was an adapter. I adapted to the situation and let the fear of the unknown keep me trapped.

One day, I was in the kitchen with my then preteen son when I made a decision that would change everything. I asked my son a question, and his response is branded into my brain. He stated "I don't know. I forget everything. I am pathetic." I was horrified! That was it for me. I had been selfishly choosing to stay in a situation and play life "safe and small," and it was impacting and influencing my son. I was done. It was now about doing what was right for my son and his future.

God has a funny way of moving in our lives. It was during this time I was introduced to a health and wellness focused network marketing company.

Along with my new energy and vibrant health, I also discovered the world of personal growth. I said, "Yes" to a company that creates the ability to impact physical pain, provides financial hope, and leaves a legacy. Through this industry and personal growth, I have realized that at a human level, what was being carried out in our home was not ok for anybody.

There are a few important lessons I gained from this experience: the importance of self-reflection, the importance of belief in ourselves, the importance of surrounding ourselves with people who are striving to grow and #BETHECHANGE. Finally, I learned the importance of network marketing. Network marketing is a personal growth plan with a compensation plan attached. It is a vehicle that pours life into your soul and a fertile environment for you to grow into your full potential. If you are in a dark space in your life, you must first recognize that something is not right. Be so dissatisfied with your situation that it propels you to an improved setting, or catapults you in a completely different direction.

My circumstance showed me that I had the strength to tiptoe into the unknown. I became OPEN to new things, new experiences, new concepts. What I was living was not serving me, my child, or anyone around me. I put on my armor, and I took a leap of faith for me and for my son and never looked back. I removed myself and my son from that environment and chose a different life, one that would not be easy, but worth it.

Because I chose to put personal growth first, to continue to be the change, literally, it has overflowed into my son. I pray that the experiences, encounters, and relationships he has witnessed will fuel and empower him on his own journey. From the Tony Robbins Youth Leadership Program to Robert Kiyosaki, Jack Canfield, Jim Rohn, Cashflow board games, and countless conversations with adults who are living conscious lives, he has witnessed positive impact on this planet. He volunteers and he reads books that most adults haven't heard of. Had I remained "suppressed," he would not have experienced the above.

Failure is only a temporary change in direction to set you straight for your next success. For all the epic fails I have had in life, I think about how I have learned to embrace becoming an overcomer. My failures have not defined me; they have propelled me. I think about how many times I have fallen and how many times I have gotten back up again. I applied to nursing school and was denied again, again, and AGAIN, for several years until I FINALLY was accepted into a program almost two hours away. Imagine if I had given up after the third denial letter or even the fourth or fifth. I was accepted after the ninth submission! Be an OVERCOMER. The only people who fail are the ones that give up.

Being accepted was only the beginning. I then had to pass, while raising a child, balancing a family, and taking care of the house. I had to commit. I had to have a crystal-clear vision of where I was going.

Then there were the multiple back surgeries, the first when I was 19 to correct progressive scoliosis. The second, was after a motor vehicle collision that produced just the right impact to snap a titanium rod in my back. It was removed. The third was a result of my spine never actually fusing and my discs beginning to degenerate. I developed scoliosis again along with lordosis and kyphosis. I felt like I was trapped in the body of an 80-year-old. They placed another rod in my back in hopes I would have relief. With each back surgery, I was being cut the full length of my back. Each time I had to teach myself how to use those muscles in my body and fight through caring for my son and putting on my shoes, only to find out I would have to endure another surgery.

My choices were to curl up in a ball, cry, and become a victim or shed my tears, put on my armor, and go into battle. Although, at the time, these events seemed so painful and useless, they have served me well even in parenting, my business, and things that I believe in. Expect failure, embrace failure, dance with failure, and learn from failure. Don't let fear of failure decide what chances you will take. Don't let continuous failure bring out your white flag. Anything worth having is worth fighting for. Don't take my word for it, look at some of the greats on this planet: Steve Jobs, Michael Jordan, Walt Disney, the Beatles, and Oprah Winfrey. Despite low moments, they have all had massive, worldwide success.

I remember the day that my son asked to live with his father. I felt defeated; ego took over my emotions and life. I thought, "Why me?... Do you know what I have done for you?" But this was not about me. It was a part of HIS own journey. My mission with my business changed too. I had made everything about my son. We lose our identity in our children but don't have to. Being a parent, a single mom, is not what defines me or you. What I know to be my truth is: my responsibility as a parent is to help my child discover what lights him up, what drives him, what his passions are and then fan those flames. My responsibility is to "tell him" the path I would prefer him to walk and tell him the kind of person I want him to be. My responsibility is to be congruent with my message and SHOW HIM who he can be when he lives unapologetically, passionately, full of life, and in service for others. My responsibility is to show him what is possible when he steps into his greater calling. His responsibility is to make his own decisions that will create his own story.

That is how network marketing has empowered me. Thanks to my freedom, I am living my life to the fullest degree. In addition to becoming a bikini fitness competitor, I am now blessed to travel on philanthropic, medical mission trips around the world and head up Smile Project, the Dallas millennial generation health and wealth creation group.

It's not about what this industry has done for my life, it's not just about what it has done for the people around me and their families, it's about the ripple effect that has been created for future generations because I had the courage to say "Yes." The strength I have pumping through my veins from these challenges is a gift. You may be thinking you don't have that kind of strength, but I assure you, you do. It is in every single person. It boils down to a decision. Will you choose you? Your bigger purpose? The pain? The failures? Will you be so dissatisfied that you demand change in your life? Or, will you settle into comfort and status quo? If you are unwilling to do it for your own life, are you willing to make a change and meaningful impact for the legacy to follow? For your children and future generations? These mountains, have trained me to wake up and start every single day expecting a challenge. But, along with the challenge, I expect bliss, joy, and memories that will last a lifetime.

TWEETABLE

Failure is a change in direction to set you up for your next success. Expect failure, embrace failure, dance w/ failure, learn from failure.

Sarah Rhew is an entrepreneur, leadership trainer, transformation coach, NPC bikini competitor, Isagenix coach, ER nurse, vlogger, and single mom. She's on a mission to bring families together, teach people how to design a dream life, and wake up society! She is passionate about helping people connect with their purpose, transform their bodies, empower their minds, achieve financial independence, and fall madly in love with their life.

Sarah@SmileProjectFreedom.com
www.SarahRhew.com
Facebook: SarahERhew
Instagram: @GlutenFreeSarah
Twitter: @SarahRhew
LinkedIn/YouTube: Sarah Rhew

CHAPTER 19

Courage Beyond the Lies

by Barb Nicholson

This summer, my husband, Jeff, and I had the privilege of hosting a multi-company appreciation picnic for the amazing people that partner with and work for us. As we looked over the crowd of smiling faces and families, I was moved to tears. We live a life beyond my wildest expectations. We truly have been blessed beyond measure!

Represented at the picnic were four companies we are partners in, that employ approximately 400 people and two additional companies that our children own and run. 28 years ago, Jeff and I were the business. We were the owners, the employees, and the everything else. Both of us were raised in families that started and ran small businesses, with all the unresolved issues and resentments that flourish there.

I grew up in chaotic and alcoholic household. Neither of our families sought or modeled a connection with Jesus. Jeff had been in the real estate development business for a decade and I was a new BBA graduate with degrees in finance and economics. I knew I wanted a family, three children to be exact. I instinctually knew there was a better way to do family, I just didn't know what it was. I figured we would work it out as we went. I was in for a whole lot of surprises!

Fast forward to two babies, four employees, home and car mortgages, less personal and relational time, and the recession of the early 90's. Add into that an employee who embezzled even our last $5000 worth of savings, after taking all the money we had scraped together for contractor payments, in our latest real estate project. We pretty much crashed and burned. My husband and I were in survival mode. We didn't have role models or mentors for our marriage. We found out how few friends we really had. I left our businesses and started my own residential real estate career to support our family, while Jeff struggled daily to keep our business afloat.

The days of taking my babies to work were over. We signed our boys up for daycare. Daycare seemed a grand adventure for our oldest son, but our youngest at the time hated it. He would cry every time I dropped him off. Then I would sit in the car and cry for ten more minutes by myself before going to work. Our young marriage was under incredible stress, and neither

Jeff nor I had ever dealt with healing from the pain in our pasts, learning healthy relationship skills, or discovering the life-changing power of faith.

We trudged through our problems and issues, suffered miscarriages, finally had another baby, kept our businesses afloat, and mutually decided I should stay home with the three little boys. Jeff was working about 100 hours per week, and I was feeling like a single parent. I had worked outside the home since I was 14 and had no concept of deriving my value from anything other than financial reward. During this time our sons were each diagnosed with ADHD, ADD, or dyslexia. School was a challenge for all our sons and hell for our youngest (to be fair, he was probably hell for school). There were countless teacher and doctor appointments, homework wars, and behavioral challenges I was ill-equipped for. Jeff and I also both came from families that taught us to make everything look "good" on the outside, the "perception is everything" crowd.

This, on top of marriage problems, landed me in clinical depression, on anti-depressants, angry, and completely shut down. I was at my own rock bottom. The good thing about the bottom is that there is only one way to go from there. Of course, I could choose to stay in the pit, or I could choose to do something different. I will save my life-altering discovery of Jesus for another time. Right now, I will just say that I would have always called myself a Christian, but I didn't really know Jesus. Jesus was and is my answer. Having the power of co-laboring with God began to change me and continues to. As I journeyed through counseling, church, and A LOT of personal work I was able to confront the lies I had believed in my life. Lies about who I was, lies about how life should be, lies about who God was, wrong ways of thinking about others, and lies I believed about marriage.

You might know these lies as the "tapes that run through your mind" telling you things like "I'm not good enough, not worthy, not lovable, not pretty enough, not smart enough. I don't have what it takes...."

My biggest lies were that I was bad (no matter how much good I did), that I could never do or be enough, that I was all on my own, and that my value was based solely on what I could do perfectly or how much I weighed. Sit with that for a minute and try to imagine how it would be to have me for your spouse or mother. Imagine the picture-perfect home and holidays I used to try to create and how much pain and stress surrounded them. I was wrapped up in knots trying to make everything and everyone look perfect. I operated out of fear, not love. These lies kept our whole family on a hamster wheel of shame, blame, and strife. Being able to confront these lies and walk with the power of Jesus allowed us to start thinking differently about life, about marriage, about raising our family, and about doing business.

Hear me that this took time, choice, process, and supportive friends to walk with. No longer do we accept the status quo or someone else's advice on principle. We don't attempt to keep up with the Joneses. We march to our own heartbeat. Now we are equipped to partner with God for answers and solutions to challenges that used to take us out. We ask a lot of questions! We learned how to forgive each other, others, and even ourselves. We learned how to fight for our marriage and our children's hearts. We learned healthy relating methods and started using "I feel…" statements instead of "you make me feel…" statements. We came completely clean in our marriage—no secrets, ever. We permanently removed "divorce" from the conversation. We decided to always be FOR each other. We were able to better discern healthy from unhealthy relationships in our lives and set appropriate boundaries.

When a problem arises, it no longer pits us against each other. Instead it is us against the problem. I learned grace and personal heart care, for myself, which allowed that to flow from me to others. We practice gratitude. Our home is the safest place on the planet for our family or anyone else that walks in the door.

We discovered how each of our children's learning styles differ and started helping them according to what works best for each one of them. Not all people and not all careers require a college or university degree. It depends on the person and what they want to do. We explored private school, homeschool, IEPs in public school, tutoring, non-conventional therapy like equine assisted learning, family small groups, and so much more.

We started making fewer judgments and way more observations. We became our own biggest advocates for our marriage, our children, our health, and our businesses. To me, this means we tried different things. We didn't join everyone else's idea. We quit making so many assumptions. We quit using labels.

We renamed ADD Adventure Deficit Disorder. We quit speaking negatively about ourselves, others, or situations. We actually did a 40-day negativity fast to kick this off. We connected with God on matters that most would not consider religious, especially in our business. We found that money is a wonderful tool but a horrible master! Generosity in crazy ways has been one of our solutions to the money problem. We realized that the more we support worthy causes with both time and money, the more peace we receive. Giving has created an abundance mindset for our whole family, plus it is just plain one of the most fun things to do! We believe that business is one of the key ways to positively impact a city. We believe that through our businesses we are making our community better. We believe as owners that we lead best through serving those that work for and with us.

We sought a legacy solution for our businesses. We came from a generation where each generation goes out on their own and starts over. We (especially me) thought this "making it on your own" and a college degree was normal and the way everyone did the "success" thing. We are discovering a better way. That our ceiling will be our children's foot stool is the desire of our hearts. This means teaching our children about business, about stewardship, bringing them into our business, and helping them start and run businesses. This means walking together and learning through the failures then getting up and doing it better.

Our goal is to create wealth and legacy for our children's children and beyond. For us that meant switching our build and sell model to a build, manage, and retain model, even as we do new things. If we only sell, we only receive cash, which has an incredible ability to disappear quickly. Income producing assets, on the other hand, create "mailbox money" or passive income. Fostering relationships with both our partners and managers has been key. Empowering others has exponentially increased our available hours in a day! They do a good job at what they do, and we do not try to micromanage or interfere with their expertise. This allows both them and us to do what we each do best. We assume if something doesn't work that we will find a better way.

Today, we still face challenges. Trouble happens. Life happens. We are people, a family, and businesses in process. Each of our children have their own story and journey. Our family is growing with the addition of two amazing daughters-in-law and a precious grandson. What has changed is how we walk through the challenges facing us. We have each other and we have Jesus. My husband truly has changed and is changing a city. Of course, he is not the only one, but his impact can be seen all over downtown Kalamazoo, Michigan. He has rehabbed countless old buildings and built new, resurrecting them into vibrant community serving offices, restaurants, retail establishments, and residential housing. Jeff is a constant mentor to our sons and countless others. He has a growing vision, servant heart, and a humble demeanor that swells my heart with love for him daily. And me? I have found the courage beyond the lies to share our journey and pursue my love of art and writing. I became a certified Soul Restoration instructor to help others clear the lies out of their lives. We are blessed beyond measure.

We all want the best for our kids, families, marriages, businesses, and cities. I suggest we start with ourselves and our homes. Find your faith. Ask God if you are believing any lies. Ask God to reveal the truth to you. If you are married be a marriage ninja and a true partner in your marriage. To me this means that your marriage isn't always 50-50, sometimes it is 60-40 and other times it is 100-0. Get healthy: emotionally, spiritually, relationally and physically. Don't follow the status quo—ask questions, learn about money, and be responsible for your children's education in both traditional and non-traditional ways. Love yourself.

TWEETABLE

Now we are equipped to partner with God and each other for answers and solutions to challenges that used to take us out.

Barb Nicholson is a daughter of the King, wife, mother, seeker of truth, artist, writer, photographer, and lover of hearts, beauty, and nature.

Barb and Jeff Nicholson started PlazaCorp Realty Advisors 30 years ago. They are owners in Heritage Guitar, The United Kennel Club, Enterprise Food Services, and a $100M plus real estate portfolio. Their sons participate in the family business and have started or are owners in Strictly Performance Motorsports, NewView Residential, and CTSV Brake Swap.

Email: nicholsonsrus@aol.com
Instagram: barbnicholson1

CHAPTER 20

Escaping the Phone Book
Breaking out of the Box!

by Laurel Boylan

One day I was meeting with a sales rep from the Fresno/Clovis yellow pages when, all of a sudden, I saw a map of my life. I was stunned to see that all three of my previous careers were on the EXACT same page! The first category I spent 14 years in was AMBULANCE. The next was ALZHEIMER's Assisted Living. The last was ADOPTIONS. What are the odds that out of 5,000 pages, all three of my career choices were on the EXACT same page!? So I jokingly perused the page to see what was next. Little did I know, I was about to bust out of those yellow pages altogether!

Fast forward to the fall of 2014. I was married and had five beautiful children, all of whom entered our family through the gift of adoption. I was running a nonprofit that my husband and I formed called God's Waiting Children, Inc. We did orphan ministries and adoption services in Ukraine. I spent my days helping families navigate the difficult, expensive, and often frustrating process of international adoptions. I also helped families learn the parenting skills needed to bond with previously broken, hurt, and abandoned children. My work with God's Waiting Children was strictly volunteer. Our family was struggling to make ends meet with seven of us living on my husband's salary. Through the stress of raising five small children, undergoing seven surgeries between the ages of 42 and 49, and trying to survive when our financial situation had been thrust into a downward spiral, I was a mess. I had gained 45 pounds and was carrying the stress of the world on my arthritic joints. I hurt, was frustrated and felt helpless, yet I continued to spend my days helping other people.

A friend invited me to try a 30-day nutrition program to help me manage my stress, lose some weight, and feel better. I agreed to try it but only to "kick start" my weight loss. I fully planned to abandon the program at the end of 30-days and continue my health journey with my own good habits. Surprisingly, at the end of the month I felt GREAT and had friends asking me how I was managing my insane, crazy life with such grace.

You see, the same month I started this nutrition program was the same month my dad had colon surgery, got diagnosed with stage four cancer, and ended up with an ileostomy bag. Four of our five kids were starting at new schools, so we had four different schools to keep up with now and all of the back-to-school details to contend with. And my mom started to exhibit signs of dementia. My husband and I decided to make the very difficult decision to move my dad into our home and care for him, which compounded the already existing challenge of raising five children. Yet, I marched on with my nutrition program that was giving me the inner strength to endure.

This nutrition program that was transforming my health was part of a network marketing company. I was approached about turning my great results into a business to help our family's financial situation. I refused to listen. I was not open. All that went through my head was, "I have five children that require regular trips to the doctor, I am running a non-profit and facilitating multiple adoptions, trying to help keep my mom safe, AND caregiving for my dad with an ileostomy bag in my home, and you want me to start a business? Are you crazy?!"

I have always been one to seek God's guidance. When God wraps His loving arms around me and leads me somewhere, I go. So, I hired a professional in-home caregiver to care for my dad, I enlisted the help of friends to transport my kids when my husband was at work, and I left my family for three days to go to an event to learn more about the company and network marketing industry. After all plans were set to attend this event, my brother informed me that we had to move Mom into an assisted living on the day I would be gone. I felt the forces working against me and trying to keep me home, inside the box, in my familiar territory of stress and caring for others.

But I BUSTED out of the box. I went to the event guilt-ridden and curious. WHY was God asking me to leave my family at this critical time? I did not have to wait long for the answer. The first day of the event was life-changing for me. One of the first stories I heard from the stage was from a lady who had adopted a little boy from Ukraine. Their adoption process in Ukraine took much longer than expected, and her husband lost his job because of it. They came home with their new child, had six other children, and were faced with financial devastation. My ears could not believe what they were hearing. This lady just told my story! This "almost millionaire" network marketer pulled her family out of financial devastation in only a few years time and dedicated her life to helping others do the same. BAAM. It hit me like a 2x4 across the forehead. I started weeping. I cried uncontrollably for an hour or more. I have never felt God's presence more than at that very moment. He set me on fire!

I came home from that event and started the process of shutting down our non-profit organization. I realized it was time to help my own family first, then reach out to help others. My dad had survived the three days without me. My kids and husband had survived. My mom got moved into assisted living despite my absence. I felt myself breaking through the co-dependent caregiving mindset and making my own health and mental sanity a priority. I was on-fire to change the course of our family's future. I had finally found the vehicle to provide ever-increasing freedom—freedom from physical pain, emotional pain, and financial pain. I found a tribe of people to help me get there.

As a mompreneur, I am fully present for my family while I earn income. Now, I am showing other people how to free themselves from physical and financial pain while I never miss one of my children's field trips or award ceremonies. Network marketing is working for myself, but not by myself. It's a way to travel and see the world, with my family by my side. It's a personal development journey. This industry taught me how to dream again. It has stretched me, and fulfilled me in unimaginable ways.

I am happy to announce that you will NEVER find me in the yellow pages again. I have built a network of team members who already have my number. I choose who I want to work with. I don't solicit for strangers to call me. I am intentional with who I surround myself with and have linked arms with people who inspire me. Being a mompreneur is a blessing from God.

TWEETABLE

When God calls, I answer! Simply being open to new opportunities can change your life. #EscapingThePhonebook

 Laurel Boylan is a wife and mother to five beautiful children. She holds an BA in journalism and a MA in business and organizational management. In 2006, she and her husband founded God's Waiting Children, Inc., a non-profit charity to assist American parents with Ukraine adoptions. Prior to that, she worked in Alzheimer's assisted living and the ambulance industry. She is now a Crystal Executive with Isagenix.

www.laurelboylan.com
Laurel@laurelboylan.com
Phone 559-321-5368
@laurelboylan

CHAPTER 21

From Beer Money to Successful Faith-Driven Mompreneur

by Brenda Fenner

The Irish say, "If you want to make God laugh...tell him your plans." Well at 18, I didn't have plans. I didn't dream of being a stay-at-home mom nor did I dream of making millions, but I'm sure grateful that it turned out I could do both!

I was excited to begin college but knew I couldn't take my retail job with me. I was trying to figure out how I could make money. It was probably the first time I looked at what my mom did as an actual "job." She had always provided really well for my brother and I, and the products she sold through her home-based business had cleared my acne. I figured other girls needed that too, so I asked her to tell me how it all worked. I remember thinking to myself, "This is so cool. If I sell one mascara, I can earn enough to buy a pitcher of beer."

I trained, went to work, and built my business that summer and then took it with me to college. Although I couldn't exactly put my finger on it, there was something intriguing and empowering about having my own business. I was having so much fun, however I still assumed I'd figure out my perfect career while in college and then find a "real" job.

But you know what they say about assuming....

I left college without graduating, and just about everyone (except Mom) said, "You need to find a "real" job with benefits." That sounded reasonable, although I noticed that most people telling me this didn't like their "real" job.

I didn't realize I had been bitten by the entrepreneurial bug, but I had tasted freedom and recognition and the excitement of being rewarded for a job well done. I liked having my own hours, meeting and making new friends, and helping them feel great about themselves. This seemed SO much more rewarding than an office job. I knew then that I'd rather be a "glad I did!" instead of a "wish I had," so I decided to take it more seriously. I had a plan!

I wish I could tell you it was all peaches and cream.

But it wasn't.

Oh, I was making plenty of money, but I would spend it just as fast in those early years. There were mornings I woke up and realized I didn't have enough to pay my rent! Because I owned my own business, I had the option to work extra hard when I needed to generate more income. It's amazing what we can accomplish when we don't have time to make excuses! I never thought I'd say it, but I'm thankful for those stressful times because that is where my confidence was built, and my business took off! I was able to support myself very nicely from age 19 to 31, all on my own, without ever having a "real" job!

At 31 I married the man on my goal poster (yes…I had a goal poster for the man of my dreams!!) Katelyn and Kyle arrived not long after that. They were just 1 & 3 when Mark was offered a promotion however we'd need to move from Kansas City, MO to Dallas, Texas. It was a big move and it was sudden, so we are forever grateful that my business had no territories. His career required travel so we were glad mine didn't. Even if I would have "planned" my perfect life I might not have ever expected to move away from our families.

Thankfully, I had mentors that continued to coach me and teach me skills that proved to be helpful not only in my business but also for me as a wife and mother.

My business kept me from getting lonely. I could work during naptime, and it was good for me to get out of my mommy clothes and spend a few hours being a professional. As women, we all deserve and could use some "me" time with friends! In the early days of our move, I was delighted to meet new, fun women, but as the kids got older, I was happy to be around to know their friends and parents too! I drove my kids to practices, games, appointments, and field trips and enjoyed every minute because I wasn't exhausted from working all day and fighting traffic. Teaching others to feel good about themselves and building my business on MY terms and MY schedule allows me to work hard and play hard. I was taught to focus 100% on my family and 100% on my career but never at the same time. Mary Kay Ash said everyone has an imaginary sign around their neck that says, "Make me feel important," and that's true with your family too!

It sounds a little counter intuitive when you first hear it…but the more you give away…the more that comes back to you. I realized my business, which later turned into my calling, was not about selling products, but fulfilling a woman's need to look and feel beautiful. A makeover could do that. Most of the ladies I know are givers, like a pitcher of water that just keeps pouring out to others. A free makeover and a little complimentary beauty advice is the beginning of refilling the pitcher. It feels awesome to empower women!

There are so many things I've learned. I figured out early on that I am not good at cleaning my house, and it does not bring me joy! I learned that, by prioritizing, I could do MORE of what I am good at and pay someone to do the things that I'm not! I love to teach other women that too! When Momma's happy, everyone's happy!

Another important lesson I like to share to prevent women from getting overwhelmed is, "Go as far as you can see, and when you get there, you can see farther."

While my original goal was to just earn a little spending money, I never dreamed the efforts I put in would lead to a life of being treated like a queen with gifts and fabulous trips! I still can't believe that I, a girl from Kansas, have travelled to the most exotic and prestigious locations all over the world! These are vacations that I never thought I would be able to experience in a lifetime! I still pinch myself at the opportunities my career has afforded us— dining ON the Great Wall of China, eating in the Great Hall of the People in Beijing, where not even local dignitaries are allowed, a private tour of the Sistine Chapel and SINGING in Abbey Road Studios! But that's just the tip of the iceberg! We were catered on hand and foot at the luxurious Four Seasons suite in places like Maui and Provence, France, and dined IN the Eiffel Tower and the Hotel De Paris in Monte Carlo. Mark and I love the water, so some of our favorite memories are parasailing above the yachts in Monaco and being part of a French sailing regatta on the Red Sea! I would do this business for free, but the added perks make it even more incredible! The thought of traveling outside the US might have made me nervous in the beginning, but I went as far as I could see, and when I got there I could see farther, and I was ready. The best part: our children have no fear about traveling the world!

Yes, it takes faith. Yes, it takes guts! My willingness to do something unique to earn a little money while in college turned out to be the answer to a question I never knew I was asking. The older I get, the more I realize we are not in control, but we have instinct for a reason! Don't deny yourself because you're scared!

So how has being a mompreneur affected our family? When you truly enjoy what you do, you exude a sense of peace, security, joy, and confidence that is reflected in your children and their decisions.

I remember the somber look our son Kyle had after school the day before all the ninth graders would be getting school issued iPads. The parents had to subsidize part of the purchase price and Kyle found that three of his classmates were probably not going to get one. Even though he didn't know these students, Kyle took on the task of raising money for all three students, working through his guidance counselor anonymously to make sure they got their iPads. Kyle is truly a compassionate leader. He doesn't do the right thing for the limelight. True character shows when you do the right thing even when nobody is watching!

I'll never forget when we had recently moved into a new home and Katelyn dropped the jar of grape jelly on the kitchen floor and it exploded onto the cabinets and the throw rugs. Without missing a beat, she looked up and said, "Mom, you're always looking for the positive, and I bet we needed to wash these rugs!" Katelyn always has that upbeat, positive attitude! She smiled, and we laughed! I'm so glad that is what she "caught" from me!

Katelyn and I laughed often even as she got older. We spent lots of time on the boat. I could usually take Kyle to baseball or basketball practice, and he'd practice with the team, but Katelyn was a competitive wake boarder, so year round I would either drive the boat or ride as she was being coached. If I was working one of those "real" jobs, I might have gotten fired for all the time I was taking off to be with my kids. Thank goodness I was the boss!

Mark and I believe that the best thing you can do for your children is to always be a shining example for them. Our kids know that it's not the clothes, the purse, the house, or the car that's important, it's who we are as people. Mark and I didn't spend a lot of time telling our children about self-confidence, taking risks, or being generous to others. As they say, "What's caught is more important than what's taught." We hope our actions showed them.

We were married for 17 years when Mark grew frustrated with his corporate job. We are so grateful for the stability and earning potential of my business. This made it easy for us to take on the risk associated with Mark leaving the golden handcuffs of a corporate job and starting a new business from scratch and enabled him to pursue his dream of owning his own business. He's been in business for five years now, and it makes me so proud to see his success and know that he has had such a positive impact on people's lives, especially the lives of his children!

So my message to you is simple. You can't give your children what you don't have. There must be more to life than just making money. You need a reason to be passionate about your life's work. And never forget, your children watch and learn from EVERYTHING you do. When mom and dadpreneurs set and exceed goals, celebrate successes, and work through the challenges together, our children learn to do the same thing.

And THAT is powerful!

TWEETABLE

When you truly enjoy what you do, you exude a peace, a security, and that will be reflected in your children.

Brenda Fenner, Senior Sales Director, helps women look and feel more beautiful by teaching skin care and color application with Mary Kay Cosmetics. She has earned 14 cars and over 50 carats of diamonds but is most proud that she's lead many others to earn them too. Her unit has women in 35 states, sold over a million dollars last year, and is ranked #5 in the world. Brenda was awarded the highest award in Mary Kay, the Ms. Go Give, for unselfishly helping others. She serves outside Mary Kay through volunteering to empower women and children.

www.brendafenner.com
214-282-9939
brenda@risepg.com

CHAPTER 22

How I Ended My Life to Find My DRIVE

by Melissa Kirkpatrick

I've been in entrepreneurship since the age of ten when I energetically sold stationary up and down the country roads around our home. My bike ride door-to-door was fueled by my desire to receive my stationary for free if I sold enough to others. I did just that.

Leaving high school, I began working an office management position, teaching adult education classes at the local vocational school, and direct selling cosmetics. I married my high school sweetheart, and we had two sons.

All was well looking from the outside. I was checking all the boxes, but I'd lost myself and couldn't see what was next.

So, I choose a different direction. Having a passion for being in direct sales, I decided to be a stay-home mom and pursue my entrepreneurship as a multilevel marketing distributor of health and wellness products.

A year passed, and I began to see that for our future we needed additional income. It was not an easy decision. I decided to return to the workforce while continuing to grow my MLM business. I was able to find a position within the school system as the secretary of the adult education program.

The position was perfect. I loved being in the school setting. As a child, I played school all the time, and having had the experience of teaching adults, I knew I was a natural when it came to teaching. I was feeling satisfied.

But when I was about to celebrate my 30th birthday, I began to question everything. Reflecting back, I discovered how I was following what I call a blueprint whereby I was adapting and being in service to what others wanted and needed but slowly releasing my own desires. Over time, being a wife, mother, employee, and entrepreneur, I was doing everything for everyone else and losing myself along the way.

Was my life what I wanted it to be at this age? Was it enough for me? What will the next 30 years look like? I knew I was in need of MORE. But more of what?

In that moment, I was ready to end my life—but not in the way you'd think. Not suicide. Just stepping out of the life I had created to look for something MORE.

I gained the courage to approach my husband and tell him of my unhappiness.

But what direction do I take? I hadn't thought much about what I'd do once I told him I was seeking change. I felt scared not really having a plan. Fear set in, and I knew I had to do something because I had opened my heart up to allow wanting more in.

Then it happened, something I know as "divine timing" today! A friend of mine called and said, "I'm going back to college to get my teaching degree!"

"Whoa. You are doing what?" I asked. And when she said it again, I was, without hesitation, hearing myself say, "I want to do that too!" My body was tingling all over, and I received my answer loud and clear.

She said, "Classes start next week."

"I'm all in." was my reply. My heart was racing, my energy was raised, and I told my supervisor, "I'm going back to school. I'm going to be a teacher."

That was my tipping point. I knew that in four years I'd be a teacher and nothing would stand in my way. Working full-time, raising the boys, and attending college full-time was my new schedule. As I look back, I can see that in that moment I clearly had found my DRIVE. I had the excitement and joy in my heart that had been quieted. I adapted and embraced fully my new journey in life.

Had I not opened my heart and spoke truthfully to my husband about my feelings, and had he not allowed me the space to process, I really don't believe I would have been open to receiving the possibility of going to college to become a teacher.

Everything was falling into place. I was thriving once again. My life was going in a direction that had endless possibilities. I was leading by example. My sons witnessed their mother reaching for her passion and desire to teach.

After completing my degree and starting my teaching career alongside my MLM business, an opportunity arose for my family to invest as owners of a golf course, which we did.

Then, seven years into my teaching, we had the opportunity to purchase a second golf course. I resigned from teaching and began my full-time career as a woman entrepreneur who purchased two 18-hole public golf courses and began to work alongside my family.

We became the family who owned and operated golf courses. Our sons began to play golf in high school and after graduation worked at the courses. And our oldest son went to college and earned his degree in golf course management. Being able to mentor and work together with our sons has been most rewarding in that we continue to watch them grow into hardworking men with a strong understanding of being their own boss and doing work that is rewarding. Not to mention, we have fun playing golf together.

Coming from a place of joy and happiness and living the life of my dreams, but still seeking MORE are the benefits of being an entrepreneur. Never did I imagine my place would be in the golfing industry. So, one never knows where the road may lead when they are ready for MORE.

As I stepped into my role as a golf course entrepreneur, now in my 40's, I found myself learning the game of golf on my own terms. This led me to teaching other women to play the game and to find their own drive to play with fun, laughter, and confidence.

Although I had left my teaching position at the high school, I found myself back in teaching as a mentor for women on and off the golf course. This was only a possibility because I was open to receive MORE. Now I am blessed to utilize the golf course to continue to grow myself and now inspire others.

From this experience of teaching others, I discovered a mindset practice that went along with playing the game of golf and life. As I further developed my understanding, I began to reflect on my own experiences and created a transformational coaching practice to support others called Find Your Own DRIVE where a simple five-step program of "Desire, Receive, Implement, Visualize, and Evolve" is taught to create and activate those dreams and goals that often get ignored. Through one-on-one activations, coaching, and group programs, my teaching continues to grow and expand as I share my experiences to support and encourage others along their journey.

What I know for sure is that we often just settle where we are, and the days, months, and years keep going by. But if you speak your truth and allow the clarity to come through for what's next, anything is possible. So, always seek MORE. And if you have to end your life to find your own DRIVE, then do that. Be open to receiving and believe in infinite possibilities because you may be surprised how, when looking back, everything aligned perfectly.

TWEETABLE
Always seek MORE and Find Your Own DRIVE. Staying open to receiving and believe in infinite possibilities. #findyourowndrive

Melissa Kirkpatrick is passionate about mentoring others on their journey to transformation. As Find Your Own DRIVE creator and founder, she offers one-on-one support, activation boosts, and group/self-study programs. Through her own struggles, which include overcoming addiction, Melissa developed DRIVE from mindset, requiring action, motivation, direction, and accountability. Melissa believes that support on the journey is where the transformation begins.

www.findyourowndrive.com
Facebook: FindYourOwnDrive

CHAPTER 23

Parenting Through the Eyes of Faith

by Gary and Cindy Mejia

Cindy and I, Gary, started envisioning our lives together in 1982, many months before we were married. We would sit at Redondo Beach in Southern California and talk through our dreams, our family, and our future children. Now we reflect on our dreams and cross them off one by one. Although during that time in our lives we were not strong Christians, we still understood the importance of raising our children in a Godly manner.

A big part of our family vision was for Cindy to work part-time, while I worked full-time. As our children started to arrive, we were very deliberate about Cindy working limited hours outside the home. Research suggests that children learn best through the modeling of others. There are many successful Bible stories about patriarchs and matriarchs using a relationship model to provide their children with the best upbringing in their own home as well. Cindy and I felt that for parents to achieve a strong relationship with their children, they must be willing to set aside quality time for them. Modeling a Godly life through daily interactions and relationships was our goal.

I worked for the Ventura County Sheriff's Department, which produced a good salary, but it fell short when it came to us owning our own home. The problem was that we were living in Southern California and, for the majority of families, it takes two good incomes to afford a home. We were short financially each week, wondering if we would have enough money to buy groceries, diapers, and formula. You can only penny-pinch and use coupons to a degree. This gets old fast.

The biggest breakthrough for us happened when we decided to spend time praying about our financial situation. After praying, Cindy and I felt it evident that we needed to relocate to an area that had affordable homes and that would allow Cindy to remain at home with two small children. We finally found a match with affordable housing costs, a police department with a great reputation and pay, and a great school district in Clovis, California.

This move gave us more financial freedom because we were able to begin to pay off bills and actually start saving money. We learned to endure eating frugally: macaroni and cheese and hot dogs. Cindy returned to the workforce after relocating, but we still had the desire to see our family vision come to pass. Once Cindy started working again, and we had to pay a babysitter, our finances didn't make sense. So, we put together a budget. We came to realize that we were not making the extra money we thought after paying the babysitter, so it was back to the drawing board. We also came to the revelation that our children would be getting their modeling and values from others, which was not necessarily what we wanted impressed on our boys. We felt that God was leading us back to our original family vision, which is what really birthed the entrepreneurial spirit within us.

Our entrepreneurial journey began when Cindy and I finally made the decision to believe in the family vision we discussed before marriage. We called it our vision from God because we needed to completely trust in God's provision and listen to Him, seeking his wisdom on how we could make this happen. As we prayed, we believed our first step of faith was allowing Cindy to become a stay-at-home mom. We knew something better had to be out there for us to provide that extra income we needed. In the past, we heard great success stories from others who worked in network marketing businesses, and many of these people enjoyed the independence of being their own boss. With two small children at home and me working shift work, we needed to make some decisions.

One evening, Cindy attended a Princess House Crystal party with my sister Leslie. It seemed to suit her personality just right. Cindy absolutely loved all the products and felt like she could never get enough of them. She signed up to be a consultant and became successful at scheduling parties because she was very passionate about the products and what she could offer the hostesses. She was very successful, and her success lasted for several years while the children were very young. Owning her own business gave her the flexibility she needed to stay at home with the boys. We were both so thankful that God brought this opportunity our way at the right time. Through this first experience, we could see the value of working in our own business together.

After my father retired from the aerospace industry, he started his own consulting company. Soon, I would begin another business venture with my father, Albert F. Mejia, called Mejia and Associates. Within a few years he asked me to join him as we ventured off into accident reconstruction and personal injury investigation. I had no idea how successful this would be!

As Cindy and I grew in our walk with God, we saw a need to put more emphasis on modeling our biblical principles in the home. Taking the boys to church weekly was important, but what about modeling prayer and reading the Bible in front of them? We knew we wanted to ensure future generations could see what an effective Christian walk looks like.

After some rough spots in our marriage, some of the best marriage advice we received was to pray for each other daily before we left in the morning and before we retired at night. We made it a habit of praying and blessing each other daily, and yes, we did this in front of the boys.

The evidence that this modeling impacted our sons can be seen in both of their lives today. Our boys recall hearing nightly that we loved them and that God had a plan and design for their life. We encouraged our sons to dream, and to express themselves, and to try things. Rick, our oldest son, dreamed of owning a recording studio. At the age of 17, he attended Central Valley Entrepreneur program and received a briefcase as a reward for a supreme job on his business plan and business presentation. He was the youngest in the class; most of the other students were in their 40's and 50's.

We believe there are three spiritual elements that are essential keys to making strong spiritual and Godly children. These elements are blessings, prayers, and fellowship.

The first key element is blessings. Blessings are critical for bonding spiritually to your children. It builds up their faith and strengthens your emotional connection, Cindy and I practiced blessings daily. We believed when we tucked them into bed was the perfect time. It became a time of closeness. One of our favorite blessings was, "May the Lord make you become everything you were created to be." Cindy liked to bless them by saying, "Remember this, there is nothing you cannot do." These are powerful and effective because it shows you believe that God has a special plan for them and that through God there is nothing they will not be able to do. Say it with all your heart and believe it in our heart, so your blessing is established in faith.

When it came time for our first son Rick to get married, as the father, I was very deliberate to plan a time when just he and I went away for a couple days. I wanted one last time as a father and son to impart words of life, spiritual truth, and wisdom. I must say I never planned on how emotional this time would be as we built a huge fire, talked, and ate dinner. After, I stood behind my son with my hands on his shoulders, and I spoke truth and affirmation over Rick as I felt inspired by God. I affirmed Rick as our son and then blessed him as he would step into marriage and now begin a new journey with the wife God had set apart for him. There were tears, hugs, and celebration as God showed up big. I would repeat this same type of blessing for Ryan with the same results. You can't even begin to estimate the power of a spoken blessing. I challenge every father and mother reading this book, be intentional about blessing your children daily.

Our boys knew they were loved; they were affirmed and knew they could accomplish anything in life they wanted. They knew we believed in them! Unfortunately, some of us have been misled by our own parents, and they have cursed us, unknowingly. Then we pass this on to our children, believing there will not be any ramifications from this. If you have ever called your child a name like stupid, fool, or any other word curse, you need to reverse this through blessing them and asking them to forgive you. If not, they will live with this curse and it may damage them emotionally as well as spiritually. You may not see the effects of the word cursing when they are young but as they grow older, these lies have ways of creeping up in their lives. If you ever catch yourself doing this, please be sure to ask them for forgiveness, even if they are very young. Then ask God to forgive you in front of them as an example. Modeling humility with repentance is a great way to teach them how to do this for themselves. Next, you can speak or pray the opposite of that word curse in a blessing over them to replace the curse. For example, "fool" would be replaced with the word wise as a blessing. I remember whenever Rick and Ryan would get in a fight and yell curses at each other. Cindy would grab them both and walk them through the process of repentance, seeking forgiveness, and blessing each other. To this day, the boys are best friends and were the best man at each other's weddings.

The second key element is prayer. While praying with your children, it is extremely important to make sure they are engaged. You can tell them, if they do not pay attention, it is like you are not here with me. I told them that God looks at the heart of a person. He sees what is going on inside. He knows whether we really believe what we are praying and if we are paying attention. He knows all things; there is nothing God does not know. As Cindy and I modeled prayer for the boy's, getting the boys to pray, was easy. They started small by praying at bedtime and meals. Whatever they prayed was alright, as it was from their hearts. We as adults need to come to God in prayer as our children do, innocent and expectant.

The third key element is fellowship. There are many aspects to fellowship but, in essence, it's caring for each other. We learned this lesson the hard way after we decided to sell the house in Clovis and move to North Idaho. I was finishing up attaching some trim on a cable barn and was about fourteen feet up a ladder when, suddenly, the ladder pulled away from the house and I fell backward. This fall changed my calling in life. I crushed my left heel, and thus, couldn't walk for months. I had reconstructive surgery on my foot, but recovery would take time.

Cindy and I drew nearer to God and our boys had to help in ways they never saw coming. The boys never gave it a second thought, we had modeled helping others our entire marriage. I would return to the police force, but during the recovery time, God got hold of my heart because now I saw my career as a call to ministry. I would later retire early and go to graduate school to become a pastor.

Cindy and I practiced fellowship and quality time during our family meals. Whenever our family was home together, we believed we needed to eat together and not in front of the television. We were deliberate about building our relationships during our meals. A meal is a place where people are relaxed and can have good fellowship with others. Even today our sons reflect back on our meal time and still cherish how special our time to catch up on the happenings of the day and new events to come was.

As Cindy and I reflect on the past 33 years, we can see the value of dreams, visions, and goals. We dreamed of the family we felt God was calling us to have. We envisioned what that would look like and what it would take to achieve it. And we set goals that would be our benchmarks along the way and that would guide us. Our sons truly are a blessing to us, and we can see how successful we were as parents and now grandparents because of the blessings they have both become to everyone around them. Writing this chapter allowed us the opportunity to ask our sons how it was to grow up a Mejia/Kraft. It was extremely humbling to hear their childhood version of the story, as humbling as it is to now witness the blessing of succession.

TWEETABLE

"I challenge every father and mother reading this book, be intentional about blessing your children daily"

Cindy and Gary Mejia, married 33 years, are successful serial entrepreneurs. While raising their sons, Rick and Ryan, Cindy made it big in a network marketing company, Gary worked as a full-time police officer, and they founded an accident reconstruction company. After heeding the call to the ministry, Cindy and Gary joined Isagenix where they share their belief that wholeness as a believer should mean in body, mind, and soul. "Honor God with your body."

garylmejia@gmail.com
cindykraftmejia@gmail.com
Facebook: /cindy.mejia.10690 and /gary.mejia.95
www.getfitchiefy.com
www.ehcc777.com

CHAPTER 24

The Stolen Family
How They Slip Away One Thought at a Time
by Sean G. Murphy

I t's so hard to ask for help, but it's killing us! For 30 years, I've witnessed families and businesses fall apart because of our thoughts or our perceptions of our own limiting beliefs. Einstein said the problems of man cannot be solved by the same mindset that created them.

There is a way out of this limiting mindset and the dream-killing conversations we have in our own mind. I found my way out at 14 years old. I didn't know my way would one day would produce millions of dollars in success. I can tell you 100% that money was the furthest thing from my mind that day. I just wanted my family back.

The most successful people will tell you they stumble on the secret of success, and then, because they don't know what they don't know, success begins to elude them. For many, it's years before they find success. I was lucky. My 0.9 grade point average didn't allow me to outsmart myself, and I was able to not only recognize the secret, I've been able to focus on it for the last 30 years.

It was a Saturday the day our family was ripped apart. I know this because my brother had a sleepover, and he was a dorm student at his school, so he only came home on weekends. That weekend he had a classmate over, which meant he didn't have to get up early and do morning chores. None of us really had a lot of friends over because they knew at some point they would have to work on the farm.

It was around noon that the unraveling started. It was then that my brother was thrown out of the "closet." A life changing process today, it was earth shattering 30+ years ago, and for my family, it was cataclysmic.

Let me back up just a bit. At the time, our family was one of a key family in our community. We were the example spoken of from the altar during sermons and were well-known in our small town. My two brothers and I were altar boys and usually served mass together. We were the pride of our mother and father, even though the look on our faces showed we despised 7:30 a.m. mass. There was a lot of "importance" that went along with the

Murphy name, which will help you understand the rest of the story.

"He's GAY!" were the words that were uttered by the "sleepover guest." The words were really more like shouted at my mother. Upon getting clarity on the statement, and as the rage began to well in her voice, my mother asked my brother, "What is he saying?" It was then, at the moment my brother said, "I'm gay," that my world collapsed. See, as the baby in the family, my older brothers were kings to me. Each had their own way of being my bigger brother. When I heard my mom shout, "I want you out of the house. I want your name changed. You are no son of mine, and you are dead to me!" my heart stopped.

Over the course of the next hour or so, during the yelling and the screaming, with me trying to get into the middle of them, screaming, "Stop Stop! This is killing me!" nothing could stop the rage in our house. See, Mom had a once a year drinking problem, at least that's how my memory recalls it, and the memories of "You are nothing. You will never be anything." still require daily focus to shut out. So when this explosion of emotion hit that day, and I was, at least I felt that I was, about to die from sorrow, I ran from the house. I didn't know what to do or where to go. I don't remember much, and I don't know how much time passed before I realized I was in the barn sitting on a bench I had made, crying.

It was at that moment I said, "I will never have another bad day!" I never went back inside that day or that night. I stayed in the barn, because I knew I didn't have to be around that screaming and yelling. It was that day that I realized I can't change others, but I can control my environment. And I vowed to do that. Over the course of the next few days, weeks, and months, the riff worsened. When the conversations turned to disowning him, getting his name legally changed, or just downright screaming that "this is not happening!," I would find a way to slip out of the house and find a place to sit with the dogs and talk with them, telling them it will be okay and will get better.

It was years before acceptance crept in, and many conversations and words of forgiveness passed from one to another. For me, I don't know if the feeling of losing my brother has ever really left. After losing my brother, who ten minutes prior was the namesake of the family, in one statement, our family was never the same!

It's moments like those that steal the unity of a family. After more than 30 years of studying the power of words and how they can be used to heal or hurt, I believe our families are stolen from us everyday because of the negative environment we put them in. From television, negative home environments, work environments, and stress-filled days, our families are stolen from us, and it's time to change that.

Just writing this and remembering that moment, my heart is racing, and my eyes are tearing up. It was a tragic day for me, and I was the lucky one because it was a life-changing day that forced a generational change in me for my family. I choose to never have another bad day, no matter what!

Now as a husband and father, the daily lessons I use with my son, Mason, have allowed me to live my mantra of better dad and better husband. I ask my bride each day if she will marry me, and most days she says "yes!" so I get to proclaim her my bride. I also ask each week, on a scale of 1-10, how was I as a dad, and I listen to Mason's answer. I have had a few 10s… but 13 year olds don't always see the life lessons being taught.

Mason knows the three rules:

1. Never disrespect your mother.

2. Say thank you and please.

3. Tell the truth, because if you lie, how can you be trusted?

I am filled with honor as I share stories about my life as a child with Mason. About how my brothers taught me so much, cared for me, and did what they could to keep me safe. When our house in Florida was destroyed by hurricanes little Mason went to Uncle Michael's for the day and cried and freaked out all day. Until, Uncle Michael put him in front of the fan, and he immediately fell asleep. Michael said, "He was HOT. That was it?!"

My brother Jimmy is the "story crafter" and I love it when Mason asks after talking with Uncle Jimmy, "Is he telling me the truth?" And I have to admit, sometimes I'm not sure!

I wouldn't change a thing about my experiences. I love my family, all of my family. We may not get to say it that often, so let me share a thought. They are your blood, there is a connection that no other human on earth has with you like your siblings. So to mine – I love you, Michael, and I love you, Jimmy and all the families.

Now, I don't believe I've been perfect over the past 30 years. But I will say I've had a heck of alot more "outstanding days" than average days. No matter the tragedy or triumph, remember it's your choice, and you can find the best in the worst. You just have to know how to look for it. I give credit to that day for allowing me to build what I have, an incredible family with my wife, Michelle, and son, Mason.

I've traveled the world in over 30 countries as a speaker and trainer, speaking to more than 750,000 people in my career. If you are like most positive households, you have had over 140,000 impressions put into your mind of negative thought! Damn! That's a lot we have to overcome, and we can't do it on our own. It's time to change that, and that's why I started my companies and my mission of daily working to be "A Better Dad and Better Husband."

TWEETABLE

If this was all there was, would this be all you would do? MentalProfits - Your Thoughts Create Your Income

Sean Murphy speaks globally on personal accountability and the three simple steps to daily success. His CQCE Formula is in demand for professionals in sales and network marketing and platform speakers because of its proven ability to create customers. It made this 0.9GPA student a global speaker, trainer, consultant.

www.seangmurphy.com
sean@seangmurphy.com
https://www.facebook.com/mentor2mentor
https://www.facebook.com/mentalprofits/
Visit https://www.seangmurphy.com/p/MomsAndDads to get your private, 30 minute "Balance Statement Review."

CHAPTER 25

Purpose Led Profit

by Donna Krech

went into business BECAUSE of my kids. I had a four-year-old daughter and was expecting my second baby when I realized I'd never have the freedom to be with them whenever I wanted, the perks I sought, like world travel with them, or the amount of income I was producing for someone else while I was working for someone else. I'd been raised in a direct sales household by a mom who taught me from the moment I could function that when God is first, family is second, and career is third, happiness and success are what ensues.

While plenty of folks who work for someone else achieve this order of priorities, I knew I needed to be employed by ME. I'd worked for others. The moment I turned 16, I got a job. I worked during college, and my husband and I moved to Texas so he could work. Due to many unhealthy addictions, he was fired, so we lived on my savings account and, eventually, had nothing. The most vivid memory I have is pushing my baby in a stroller down a dirt road to buy her milk, hearing the last money I had on earth jingling in my pocket (the operative word is jingling). I was sobbing, having no idea how I was going to feed her the next time she was hungry. I had to get a job.

First I sold weight loss, then fitness. I was good at both! I had a gift for generating profit! We moved back home to be with family. Eventually, I got into weight loss again. Due to wanting the freedom I mentioned earlier, I opened my own facility. I was even better at it now! See, there's a thing you know how to do that no one has taught you...that's your gift, your calling, your anointing. And I was in mine! Part of it was marketing and sales. I'm good at it. But, I was really good at generating profit!

At first, I called purpose "Healthy-Selfish" I wanted to have time with my kids and I was immovable on that. I focused on purpose at home. Some people say, "Quantity doesn't matter. Kids just need quality time." I disagree. Kids need your time! I knew I wanted to give my kids as much of my time as possible. And, when you have quality at work, you can have quantity at home.

Then Came Purpose Led Profit

While praying and doing our bedtime ritual one night, it occurred to me, people probably didn't know how to have bedtime rituals with their kids. I started teaching purpose to my team and raised my children around my companies so they all grew to understand the stuff in life that matters isn't stuff, and making money in business is simple. Here's the thing, having only purpose, or having only profit, isn't enough for true happiness and real success. You need both. I've lived and breathed this way of life for years and have now owned three nationwide companies DEDICATED to teaching business leaders how to have REAL success: to have the time, money, and energy for the stuff in life that matters to them, to have quality at work and quantity at home, to live "Healthy-Selfish."

People have asked why it wasn't enough to simply have this life for myself. It's because I knew if having purpose AND profit were important to me, it was important to others. And I knew I could teach people how to get both. How did I know? Let me explain where this came from. It will help you understand why I'm so passionate about spreading this message.

I was raised by a Stanley Home Products branch manager. She made, basically, commission only. And she always taught me that God would take care of us. My daddy had passed away when I was 15. The furnace went out, and it was winter. We didn't have money to fix it. She kept telling me, "God is going to take care of us." Within days, she went to the mailbox and found a check from social security for money that had come from my daddy passing away. It was the exact amount that we needed to fix the furnace. That's purpose. It only takes a minute to tell I'm a woman of faith, and stories like that are the reason why. I lived so many things like that. Hence, I believe! That's purpose.

I have a big, amazing family. In the last year of Mom's life, when she was very ill, we all took care of her 24/7. If a family member couldn't take care of her, I praise God that I was blessed to hire someone to care for her. That's purpose and profit.

Always Market with a "Thank You"

My mom was with Stanley for 65 years. She never quit, even at the end of her life. I was taking care of her one day, and the phone rang. I answered. The woman said, "Is this the Stanley dealer?"

I replied, "This is the home of a Stanley dealer."

She said, "I want to order some stuff."

I leaned into my 90-year-old mom's ear, "The lady on the phone wants to order some stuff. Do you still have stock in the back? Here's what she wants."

She said, "If I don't have it in the back, we'll just put in an order. Just get her information."

So, I took down all the lady's information and went back to where Mom kept her inventory. At one point, when I was growing up, this was kept in a big garage. Now, it was simply in a cupboard. I opened it and checked the inventory list in my mom's handwriting. I went back to her and said, "Mom, we have the stuff."

She said, "Alright, get me a pen." With her hands barely able to write, she wrote a handwritten thank you note.

She said, "Get me a catalog because we have to send her a catalog. And, go get a prize, we have to send her a thank you gift for placing an order." She was 90 years old, and still marketing with a "thank you." That's purpose and profit.

I also learned that selling is serving. Connected and invested are not mutually exclusive. You need to build relationships, and you need to be selling. You need to sell and build relationships. It's not one or the other. If you're building relationships and you believe in what you've got, you should be sharing that aka selling. If you're selling, you should be building relationships so there can be a lifelong connection. I learned that from her. Selling is serving. If you have something that will change somebody's life, and you don't sell it to them, shame on you. There's no part of me that thinks selling is sinning. That's purpose and profit.

Life's Short: Don't Miss a Minute of It

One of my last memories is of kneeling down in front her and holding her face in my hands. I asked, "Mom, do you know who you are to me?"

She said, "I'm your mom!"

I said, "But do you know who you really are to me?"

She said, "I don't know what you mean."

I said, "You are my favorite person."

She said, "You're my favorite person!" I could have gotten all caught up in that, but I realized it really wouldn't have mattered who was sitting there, because no matter who it was, she still would have said, "You're my favorite person." That's how she made everybody feel. If you met her right now, she could make you feel like you were her favorite person.

May I encourage you today to tell someone they are your favorite? Tell 10 someone(s)! Don't miss the moment to hold their face in your hands. That's purpose!

So, this is where Purpose Led Profit came from. From being raised by her.

I grew up watching it lived in front of me every single day. Knowing where it came from helps you understand why I am so driven to share it. She did big things in her business, and she touched people's lives amazingly. They weren't mutually exclusive; she did both. That's Purpose Led Profit. I believe you and I are called not only to profit in our business, but to also have purpose in our lives. Not only to have purpose, but to profit. And I know I'm here to teach others how to do this. And I'm the best in the world at teaching it. I believe that. That's purpose.

TWEETABLE
The Stuff in Life that Matters Isn't Stuff. Success is Having Time, Money and Energy for the Stuff that Matters to You #purposeledprofit

Entrepreneur Extraordinaire, Bestselling Author and International Speaker Donna Krech has a 30+ year record of building multimillion dollar companies and is the #1 authority on Purpose Led Profit. She has lived the American dream AND is an expert in teaching others to do the same. Her impactful message, proven success methods, and result-producing programs have triggered audiences in 94 countries to hail her a thought leader, business builder, and life changer.

www.facebook.com/DonnaKrech
www.donnakrech.com

CHAPTER 26

Leaving the World Better Than When We Found It

by Simon Chan

'll share a secret with you. Money doesn't motivate me. I get pitched all the time about new opportunities with amazing pay plans and how much money you can make. Little do these people know that money and "how easy it is to make a lot" doesn't drive me at all. Fulfillment and making a difference in this world is what motivates me. I've made many decisions in life where money is not even a top five factor. 'Cause you see, I grew up with money.

My parents went from rags to riches and achieved the American dream. I grew up in an upper middle class family and was always the richest kid in my school. My parents drove me to school in a Mercedes while other kids had to take the school bus. In fact, I grew up with three different Mercedes in our garage and driveway, and I never needed to get a job in school. As long as I was a good boy and got good grades, my parents would give me a nice allowance, and I could buy all the toys I wanted. My parents paid 100% of my $125,000 tuition so I could just study and have fun in college.

Yet, I wasn't happy. All the money in the world didn't make me happier than the other kids. What I wanted as a kid was to spend time with my dad. I wanted him to play catch with me, take me to Yankee Stadium for baseball games, and watch basketball games at Madison Square Garden. Unfortunately, he was always too busy as a doctor. He had a successful medical practice, and he was always busy at the hospital, his office, or making the weekend rounds at the nursing clinic.

I ended up spending many weekends at my grandparents, and as I reflect back, I have more memorable moments with my grandparents than with my parents. I still remember my late grandmother taking me to my first Yankees baseball game where we sat up in the upper deck and watched my Yankees win 4 - 0 against the Cleveland Indians. Our bad seats didn't matter. I was just so happy to be at Yankee Stadium watching my Yankees live.

Unfortunately, I don't have many of those moments with my dad, and I made a promise early on that I wouldn't be like that to my kids. This is in no way to say I don't love my dad, nor do I resent what he did. I totally understand why he had to do what he did, and I'm grateful that he did everything to allow my brother and me to live a comfortable life growing up. But I made it one of my goals not to follow my dad's footsteps.

Money is important, but more important is time with your kids and creating memories. I recently read a post from a young leader that said "Experiences are greater than cars or watches" and I couldn't agree more. When we are on our deathbed, what makes us happy is to think back to the memories we have with our loved ones. We don't reflect on our nice cars and watches. Life is about memories, and the more experiences we create, the more abundant our life is.

And that's what motivated me to become an entrepreneur. Because after I read *Rich Dad Poor Dad*, I realized that I would be going down the same path as my father. The only way I could create memories with my future kids would be to have a passive income stream that would continue to pay me even when I didn't feel like working.

But passive income from where? There were many options to create passive income, and I was thinking about opening up a Subway sandwich store in Los Angeles, but then I read *Purpose Driven Life* by Rick Warren, and my life changed forever. After doing the 40 days of exercises, I learned that God's purpose for me was to have a "positive impact on as many lives as possible."

I then asked myself, what type of business would allow me to have a positive impact? And that's how I decided to start a network marketing business. Because I discovered that MLM is not a sales business, but a coaching and training one. If I really wanted to build an MLM empire that'd give me the residual income to stay home and create memories with my family, I must coach and help as many of my team members as possible. I would be forced to have a positive impact on the lives I come across, and that fit perfectly with my purpose-driven life.

MLM Nation

God spoke to me again in 2012, and I decided to retire from my MLM business to become a full-time business coach, speaker, and online marketer. It also led me to start MLM Nation, a generic training company that includes the #1 rated training on iTunes. At the time, I was blessed to have built a six-figure residual MLM business that had over 80,000 distributors. I didn't need to work anymore and was already a stay-at-home dad and building memories with my first son. We would go running together with the jogging stroller a few times each week, have baby gym sessions twice a week, and spend at least one day a month in Disneyland.

But then I realized, I had made a huge positive impact with my downlines and, to a lesser extent, to other distributors in my company. But my company was only a small pond in the huge ocean called direct selling. There are over 100 million people out there in this amazing profession that still needed my help. I had made a positive impact, but not "on as many lives as possible." I still had much work to do.

And that's what drove me to start MLM Nation and go full-time as a generic trainer. The cool thing is that all the coaching and training materials are done online through webinars, Facebook groups, Skype, and emails, so I don't travel much and I get to spend time with my family. I get to pick up and drop off my kids at school and read to them every night before I put them to bed.

My Three Beliefs About Network Marketing

I'm loud and proud to be a network marketing profession because of three beliefs.

1. **MLM Allows Us to Fulfill Our Unlimited Potential**
    God has blessed every one of us with amazing abilities, but unfortunately, due to our upbringing, we stopped believing we can do much in life. You can see this when you compare a two-year-old versus a ten-year-old. When they're two, they believe they can do anything in the world, but by the time they turn ten, they've given up on many things and only do the things "they think they can do." By the time someone turns eighteen, all their dreams have died, and they live according to a fixed mindset which means "that's the way I am" or "I can't do that cause I'm not that type of person." The best part of network marketing is that if you really want to be successful, it'll force you outside your comfort zone and you'll be able to do things that you never thought were possible.

    I had low self-esteem growing up as a kid because I spoke with a lisp and a Chinese accent. I believed because of my poor English I could never speak as well as my Caucasian friends. But thanks to network marketing, I came to understand that I could do much more than I believed I could. Today, I love speaking to huge groups and being the host of the #1 rated MLM podcast on iTunes.

2. **MLM Allows Us to Give Back More**
    This amazing profession also allows us to give back more of our time and money. As we grow in this profession, we learn that true happiness comes not by how much we receive and make but by how much we give. We give more time to help our communities and charities and also donate more money. Some of my most memorable moments in the last few years are the day I was able

to increase my giving to my church and the Saturdays I spent scrubbing the walls and lockers of a local elementary school.

And I'm super excited today! As I'm writing this, I volunteered to be the assistant coach at our community tee-ball team, and this afternoon will be our first practice. Nothing beats the feeling of giving back and knowing that you're making a difference in the lives of others.

3. **MLM Allows Us to Be Better Parents Because We're Always Leading by Example**

    What type of legacy do you want to create? An easy way to create a legacy is to have your kids become better than you are. I'm grateful for this profession because it has allowed me to become a better parent. Before MLM, my kids would have grown up with TV and would have lived with a cynical and negative dad, because that's the way I was.

Each day I had to watch my ESPN, daily news, and music videos and also complained every time things didn't go my way. But network marketing taught me to work on my dreams instead of watching someone else fulfill their dreams.

It also taught me the fundamental principle of leadership which is to never criticize, complain, or condemn. Today I'm probably one of the most anti-TV people out there. We don't have a TV in our house, and our kids don't watch DVDs on long car rides. Instead, they learn to read books or carry a long conversation. We also preach and live in an environment of positivity.

Our Chan boys have to follow these 11 rules in our house.

1. Love God
2. Love and respect your parents
3. Love and respect your family
4. Have a positive attitude
5. Always be grateful
6. Be a good, loving, and caring person
7. We are always learning and getting better
8. We live healthy lives by sleeping, exercising, and eating well
9. We always hustle and work hard
10. We are calm but act quickly
11. Never never never never never give up

These 11 rules are all things that I've learned in my success journey, and I'm grateful that MLM taught me these lessons that I can now pass on to my kids. There's a saying that our children determine how successful we really are. It's not about how much money you've made when we leave this earth, but did we leave it better than when we found it? Our values get carried on by our children and are how our legacy is created.

Two Special Gifts for Each of My Three Sons

MLM has given me the time to write a book and produce a movie for each one of my boys. Before I go to bed each night, I write to all three of my kids. It's my daily diary to them where I write down the memories of the day and my love for them. At the same time, I'm also producing a movie for all three of them. I take a one second video clip each day and compile the daily highlights into a movie. So far, my oldest son's movie is over half an hour long, and his book is over 300 pages already. I plan to do this every day of their lives until they turn 18. That would be my gift to them when they become adults. The books and movies are all saved on Google Drive and even if something happens to me and I don't live until they turn 18, they will grow up knowing that their daddy loved them very much.

What's Your Purpose and Beliefs?

I've shared with my purpose driven life, my three beliefs about MLM, and what motivates me. So what drives you? What's your purpose and what do you believe in? You must be clear about your purpose because it's the ultimate driving force in your success journey. You will go through tough times, and during those moments, the only thing that is going to keep you going is your purpose. Just remember to jump outside your comfort zone to achieve your full potential, give back more, and invest time in your kids, because how they turn out will determine your legacy and whether you lived a successful life.

Thanks for being part of this amazing profession and never never never give up!

TWEETABLE
We're in the profession to help others, so go out there and have a positive impact on someone's life today

Simon Chan is the Founder of MLM NATION including the #1 MLM training on iTunes. He's a business coach, speaker, and online marketer who helps network marketing distributors find more prospects, sponsor more people, and create duplication. Prior to becoming a full-time coach, Simon built a network marketing business with over 80,000 distributors in over 18 countries and is a Million Dollar Club member.

www.MLMNation.net
www.facebook.com/mlmnation
www.facebook.com/simonwchan8899

CHAPTER 27

Finding Your Path

by Kyle Wilson

W e had mastered the formula. We would go into a new city four times a year promoting an event with two speakers using Brian Tracy, Og Mandino, or Jim Rohn. That gave us plenty of time to get moved in, set up, book our calendar full of speaking engagements, fill a huge room for an event, and then afterwards have two weeks to celebrate and be on to the next city.

It had taken four years of me being a promoter to go from modest numbers of a few hundred people to now getting 2,000-3,000 people consistently. And the major shift came when I talked my wife, Heidi, into joining me. She had never been in sales, had never used the phone to book appointments, and for sure had never given presentations to companies and then sold them at the end on going to a seminar. "That's a crazy idea," my friend Gordon told me when I suggested the missing piece to my seminar business was to recruit my wife to leave her secretarial job and join me. But that is exactly what I did, and she came on board, learned the process, and was a superstar.

We left Sacramento March of 1993, after one of our all-time best events with Brian Tracy and Jim Rohn, and headed to our next city, Kansas City. And in Kansas City, a whole series of events would change everything.

Heidi wasn't feeling well. Sick in the mornings. Dizziness. All the classic signs of pregnancy. That wasn't the plan. But indeed, she was pregnant. We went from surprise to excitement, joy to, candidly, being nervous of the unknown.

Not long after we learned she was pregnant, we received the call, my dad had a stroke and was in a coma. We made the drive from Kansas City to Dallas (Heidi was too sick to fly). My dad would pass away the day after we arrived. I felt his presence at the funeral like never before. It broke my heart he would never see and know his first grandchild.

Throughout the entire Kansas City event, it was a struggle. Heidi was sick the whole time and not able to work. And I was grieving the passing of my dad, needing to be there for my wife, and still needing to fill the room and put on a world class event.

The day finally came. The event was great but not nearly as successful as the previous three or four events.

At the end of the event, I met with Jim Rohn. He and his business partner had split up. There was a huge financial loss involved. It was that night that I made Jim an offer for me to launch Jim Rohn International.

After Kansas City, Heidi and I knew she could not continue her role while pregnant and for at least a good period of time after giving birth. I also now had an opportunity to partner full-time with the best speaker in the world (that's how I saw Jim). So we walked away from the seminar business, and I went full-time launching JRI.

Within the first 12 months, I took Jim from 20 dates at $4,000 each to over 110 dates at $10,000 each (and eventually $25,000 per talk). Also, I went to work on a product line including creating and launching a viral quote booklet that went on to sell over six million copies.

While building JRI and eventually launching YourSuccessStore.com and starting multiple publications in 1999 when the internet was taking off (I built a list of over one million subscribers), I was also raising a family.

Rebekah was born in December of 1993. Heidi wanted a natural childbirth (no drugs and a midwife). Her commitment to making the best environment for our kids was always her top priority!

March of 1996, we had our second child, Daniel. Again she chose a natural childbirth, and this one from home.

Heidi was a full-time mom and staying with the kids.

On my end, business was exploding. Before long, I had 20 employees and also was doing two-day weekend seminar events all over the country with Jim Rohn and special guest Mark Victor Hansen. And in 1996, I did a tour with Brian Tracy on a two-day event called the Success Mastery Academy, a program he and I co-created. (In fact, Brian and I did the 20-year anniversary of the program in May of 2016 with my good friends Darren Hardy, Vic Johnson, and others as special guests.)

The wear and tear was tough on our relationship. There wasn't enough of me to go around it seemed.

In 1998, I decided to get small. I did a big downsize of the company, and I moved my office to five minutes from the house. I added a full-time road person to travel to the events where I booked Jim and other speakers I was now also representing. My goal was to avoid travel and being away from home as much as possible. I made a commitment to never miss a school or sporting activity that my kids were involved in. I also signed up as coach or assistant coach when possible.

In 2001, I decided to have my first big event in several years. A three-day event with Jim Rohn in Dallas. I would invite multiple speakers and also film it. There would be no travel, but there would be a major commitment of time and energy and also a very small staff.

During the marketing of the event, Heidi started dealing with depression. I was clueless on how to help her. I was a fixer, a problem solver, but with her and this new challenge she was going through, I was helpless.

Over the next 12 years, she dealt with depression on and off. It was scary, and all my remedies did not work. She saw counselors and tried multiple approaches.

In 2007, the opportunity presented itself for me to sell my companies. The person wanting to buy me also was buying *Success* magazine. I saw this as an opportunity to press the reset button, and everyone would win. The speakers I represented including Jim Rohn, Denis Waitley, Chris Widener, and Ron White would benefit from *Success* magazine and also the direct selling companies the buyer worked with. And my team of 20 staff members would benefit from the 20% profit sharing plan I had in place and would not only keep their current level of salary but also get a windfall check. And me, I could be full-time at home with my wife and kids who were 12 and 14.

As perfect as it all sounded, it didn't all go perfectly. I was required to stay on for a year. That transition year was hard and taxing, much harder than when I owned the company. And for the team and speakers, they also had some curve balls with the transition.

In many ways, I deal with regrets about selling the company, but I also had the amazing opportunity to be with my kids full time for the next five years and to be a Mr. Mom so Heidi could go and do work she wanted to do. No matter what, I know I'm a better person for having hit the reset button.

In 2014, our youngest graduated high school. Heidi and I had been struggling greatly in our marriage for years, despite me selling my company and being home full-time. We both wanted our marriage to work for our kids and for a legacy for our family. But reality was setting in. We had tried everything, and we were struggling. We both felt we had compromised and diminished ourselves so much to make the other happy. We discussed divorce. Heidi felt she needed to spread her wings and took a job that required her to travel. During her times away we both seemed to do better. It was like our trial separation. Was it possible even some of her depression was the feeling of being trapped? We finally had the courage to talk to our kids, and we all agreed her and I might be better off going separately to pursue our life callings.

When I shared with all my friends, who all love Heidi, they unanimously said they agreed, that no one had tried harder than her and me to make it work. We had been married 27 years. But now was time.

I'm proud to say we handled our divorce in a very good way. We had one attorney, agreed on everything being split 50/50, and did a non-contested divorce. We still talk by text or phone almost daily and have continued to spend holidays and our kids birthdays together as a family. We both are happier and have a great relationship with each other and our kids. We have made better friends than partners and are in 100% support and love for the other.

Here are some lessons I've learned, in some cases the hard way, I want to share.

There is no right or wrong way for you to follow. You have to find your unique path and let go of doing things to please others or to keep up with appearances. That's one of life's test. To find your own path.

Our kids and spouses are our teachers. They know how to trigger us, just like we trigger them. Use those experiences to observe and make needed changes versus reacting.

Our kids are not us. They get to find and live their own unique path. They are not here to please us. We should not take it personally when they go a different path than we think they should. Because it's not personal. It's about them.

Shame and guilt keep people from the freedom to be who they are. As parents and spouses, we need to avoid shaming and guilting others.

We all are learning, growing, and making mistakes. Don't expect more from others than you do yourself.

We cannot fix another person. Everyone has their own unique challenges, and they have to take responsibility for themselves. You can create the best possible environment. You can pray. You can support. But, ultimately, people are responsible for their own happiness.

One of the greatest gifts we can give our family, friends, and people in our lives is respect and support for them to have their own beliefs, whether we agree or not. In fact, we may learn they see something we don't.

Judge less, support more. Seek to understand. You don't have to agree. But do give the honor and respect of letting others have their opinions and beliefs.

Lastly, I'm honored to be one of many great stories in this book. Find the stories that resonate with you and pull from them. Be inspired, be warned, be encouraged. The reason I speak boldly about depression, work stress, and divorce is that these are real issues, and there is no shame ever. Failure is only in the eyes of how people interpret things. Life and people are a gift. Live, learn, grow, love, and flow into your purpose!

Much love, Kyle

TWEETABLE

We all are learning, growing, and making mistakes. Don't expect more from others than you do yourself.

Kyle Wilson, Founder of Jim Rohn International, YourSuccessStore, LessonsFromNetwork.com and KyleWilson.com. Kyle has filled big event rooms and produced 100s of programs including titles by Jim Rohn, Brian Tracy, Zig Ziglar, Denis Waitley, and recently the books Passionistas, The Little Black Book of Fitness *and* Mom & Dadpreneurs. *Kyle leads the Kyle Wilson Inner Circle Mastermind and The Kyle Wilson Mentoring Group and is the author of* 52 Lessons I Learned from Jim Rohn and Other Great Legends I Promoted *and co-author of* Chicken Soup For the Entrepreneur's Soul! *Go to KyleWilson.com/ connect to download Free books and audios and to connect on social media.*

KYLE WILSON'S LESSONS FROM NETWORK

A Community Connecting Life and Business Experts with the Marketplace!

Here is a Sampling of the Powerful Programs You Can Access on Topics including Marketing, Selling, Branding, Speaking, Leadership, Communication and more!

Brian Tracy
Success Mastery Academy

Darren Hardy
Productivity Secrets of Super Achievers

Erika De La Cruz
Assume Your Throne

Delatorro McNeal
Crush the Stage Explode Your Income

Seth Mosley
Parents Basement to Winning a Grammy

Nick Bradley
Habits of a Champion

Roy Smoothe
You Are Your Brand

Vic Johnson
Become the Celebrity Authority

Kim Somers Egelsee's Confidence Building Course
(4-part series)

Heather Christie's Executive Leadership Coaching Model
(4-part series)

Eric Lofholm's Sales & Prospecting Persuasion & Influence
(17-Part Series)

Chris Widener's Leadership Series
(7-part series)

Vic Johnson's 4 Basics of Building a Online Business
(4-Part Series)

Bob Donnell's Mastering Your Inner Game
(7-part series)

Tony Teegarden's Client Conversion Clinic
(4-Part Series)

Ron White's Memory in a Month
(34-Part Series)

Plus Access the LFN Resource Center, Expert Calls and Live Q&A Calls!

Plus Bonus Section including Ron White's Speed Reading, Robert Helm's Unlock True You Goal Setting, Kyle Wilson & Larry Thompson's Tribute to Jim Rohn and more.

Receive a 2 Week All Access Trial to the Lessons From Network For Only $11.96
Go to LessonsFromNetworkTrial.com

About the Author

Kelli Calabrese is a student of life. She wakes up daily seeking betterment and ways to provide the same for others. With a background in wellness, she aims for spiritual, physical, financial, relational, professional, emotional, environmental, and intellectual health. In different seasons of her life she has been cast deep into challenges which she has used to strengthen her.

When Kelli was 21 she was a victim of a high-speed pursuit, broadsided and left with injuries to her spine, head, and knee. That experience sent her on a personal quest to further understand physical rehabilitation and wellness which helped her have empathy for her clients and come to understand the body mind and spirit connection to healing. Professionally, her heart and soul were deeply engrained in health club ownership, corporate fitness center management, and running a school. When pregnant with her son, she realized that it was time to change her environment so that she could have a better connection with her children during that season of raising babies. She poured her love for her profession into parenting while still finding ways to contribute to her industry. A cross-country move left Kelli and her husband with two large homes and unemployed in a new town where they knew no one. That was not only a lesson in being resourceful financially but also a time to press in spiritually and rely on something great than herself.

Each hard time, each failure, each shift in seasons had a purpose, and she used it to become stronger. She has been electrocuted and struck by a drunk driver. Her home was flooded twice. She's lost a parent and best friends, and she's faced betrayal, disappointment, and rejection. Her philosophy of being "discipled up" has served her so that when one thing happens, the other areas of her life are strong, and the situation does not have to be a crisis.

Yes, she has accomplished much in her career from media tours on every major network to being published in thousands of articles, speaking on stages to thousands, authoring books, and being a fitness expert for celebrities. However, the thing she values the most is her family and loving and training them well so that they can go out and be difference makers in the world in positive and far-reaching ways.

Kelli Calabrese: Co-Founder of Mom & Dadpreneurs: Success Stories, Strategies and Tips from Super Achievers in Family & Business

Do You Want to Accelerate Your Success in Becoming a Mom or Dadpreneur?

I hope you enjoyed and were inspired by this book.

If you are convinced or even intrigued that you can be a mom or dadpreneur with executive pay, you are a step closer to turning your dreams into reality.

You have the dream! Now let's put it into action!

I have the blueprint to get you there. My passion is teaching you how to uncover your vision, identify why it's important to you, unpack the steps to get there, and watch the transformation happen as you step into a lifestyle of purpose.

When you cast your vision, you can connect to it, capture it, create it, and ultimately, celebrate it. Everyone can do this.

I'd like to invite you to accelerate your success by watching this **free** Vision Casting Video and Activation Guide to help you bridge the gap to making your family and financial freedom a priority and reality.

Your vision for your most excellent and ideal life awaits. I'm here to help. Get into action!

www.KelliCalabrese.com/freevision

Receive Your Free Vision Casting Video and Activation Guide Now!